Paul Dobson and Gillian Morr
Rose was formerly a member)
Department of the Polytechnic

PAN MANAGEMENT GUIDES

Other books in the series:

PAN MANAGEMENT GUIDES

Essential Law

Paul Dobson
Gillian Morris
Pauline B Rose

A Pan Original
Pan Books London and Sydney

First published 1987 by Pan Books Ltd
Cavaye Place, London SW10 9PG
9 8 7 6 5 4 3 2 1
© Paul Dobson, Gillian Morris, Pauline Rose 1987
ISBN 0 330 29777 5
Phototypeset by Input Typesetting Ltd, London SW19 8DR
Printed and bound in Great Britain by
Cox and Wyman Ltd., Reading

Contents

Part One
The Business as a Company

1 Introduction and Incorporation

What follows does not seek to be a definitive or comprehensive account of the whole of Company Law but rather an attempt to identify and explain those areas which are likely to be of interest to and to affect the small businessman or manager involved in the running of a limited liability company. In the light of the volume of recent legislation – a consolidated Companies Act, a new edition of the City Code on Takeovers and Mergers and the Insolvency Act 1986 – it is all too easy for the businessman to feel drowned by the morass of detail but it is essential not to lose sight of basic principles. This guide concentrates on the areas of law which are particularly relevant to the private limited company – that is, the company in which members of the general public do not purchase shares, as opposed to the public limited company or P.L.C. in which they do. All references are to the Companies Act 1985 unless otherwise stated.

1 Incorporation

Generally someone starting a new business will begin as a sole trader or in partnership with another. Sooner or later, however, the question whether to incorporate that business as a limited liability company is certain to arise.

1 *Advantages and Disadvantages of Incorporation*

As long ago as 1897, the case of *Salomon* v. *A Salomon & Co. Ltd* established that where a business has been legally incorporated as a limited liability company, then that company has a legal existence quite independent of its shareholders. The company is a distinct legal entity.

The principle of limited liability may prove useful to the person running a business which might, at some point, have a claim made against it for damages or compensation – as in a business providing defective goods or services. Provided that the shareholders of the company have paid at least the full nominal value for their shares, there can be no claim against individual shareholders. Any claim would be against the company in its corporate name. It is true that in some transactions the directors of a limited company may be required to give personal guarantees, particularly if the company is seeking to borrow money, but such personal guarantees should be resisted if at all possible.

The directors of the private limited company are often also the only shareholders but the company may issue additional shares to existing or new investors in order to raise further capital for expansion and development.

Limited liability has the drawback of requiring certain company information to be publicly disclosed. Each year the company must file certain documents, together with the necessary fees, with the Registrar of Companies at Companies House (see Chapter 4). The Companies Act 1985 lists over forty different matters which, if they occur during the life of the company, must be notified to the Registrar – for example: changes in directors; changes to the Memorandum or Articles of Association; changes in shareholders. These documents are open for inspection by the public.

The approximate cost of incorporating a limited liability company is £300, which includes Value Added Tax and Stamp Duty, although it may be cheaper to buy an 'off the shelf' company from a company formation agent. (See page 12.)

2 Procedures for Registration Leading to Incorporation

Having decided to form a limited liability company, the businessman must comply with the formal legal requirements for registration and incorporation. He must choose a name for the proposed company which must not be the same as one already on the Register at Companies House (C.A. 1985, s.26). Additionally, he must register the Memorandum of Association of the proposed company, which must be signed by the two original subscribers (shareholders) of the company. Every limited company must have a minimum of two shareholders (C.A. 1985, s.2). Particulars of the first directors and secretary of the company and the address of the Company's registered office must also be submitted for registration, together with a statutory declaration that all requirements of the Companies Act relating to registration have been complied with. That statutory declaration must be made either by a solicitor engaged in the company formation or by a person named as a director or secretary of the company.

There is no legal requirement to file Articles of Association for the proposed company, although if none are submitted then the model set of Articles, known as Table A, will be deemed to apply to the Company (see page 19). At the time of registration of these documents a fee of £50 is payable to the Registrar. If the Registrar is satisfied that all the requirements relating to registration have been complied with, he must issue a Certificate of Incorporation giving the date of registration and allocate a registered number to the new company. Once the Certificate is issued, it is conclusive evidence of registration and the company exists as a separate legal entity from that date. The Registrar may, however, refuse to register or issue a Certificate of Incorporation for a company formed for an illegal purpose (C.A. 1985, s.1 and *R* v. *Registrar of Joint Stock Companies 1931*).

In practice, the time involved in checking the Register and submitting the forms and the often lengthy delay in the issuing of the Certificate of Incorporation may prove unsatisfactory to the businessman who wants his limited company urgently. It may therefore, be advisable for him to purchase an 'off the shelf' company, either directly from a company formation agent or through his professional advisers – his solicitor or accountant.

An 'off the shelf' company is one which has been previously registered and incorporated and held for sale by the formation agents. The clerks in the office of the agents will be named as the two original company subscribers. Such agents have several hundreds of these companies available for purchase and the approximate cost of £130 includes copies of the company documents, the company seal and the statutory books. Although the name and certain provisions in the Memorandum and Articles of such a 'ready made' company may not fit precisely the purchaser's requirements, they can be changed (see page 19) but the businessman may find it galling to discover that the Registrar charges £40 to register a change of name! On purchase, the two original subscriber shares will be transferred to two new shareholders.

3 *Memorandum of Association*

Every company limited by shares must have a Memorandum of Association which gives external information about the company and its activities (C.A. 1985, s.2).

There are five compulsory clauses which must be included in the Memorandum (six, in the case of a P.L.C.). Although some older companies may have included additional clauses, the Memorandum of most modern companies contain only the five compulsory matters which are as follows:

1 *The name of the company plus the word 'limited'*, (C.A. 1985, s.25) in the case of a private company. Public companies must add the letters P.L.C. after the name. When choosing the company name, the businessman should note that the onus is on him and his advisers to ensure that the name is acceptable to the Registrar. The proposed name must not be the same as one already on the Register, nor must it constitute a criminal offence or be offensive (C.A. 1985, s.26). If the name gives the impression that the company is connected with the Government or any local authority, the approval of the Secretary of State is required. However, the abbreviations 'Ltd' and 'Co.' in the company name are acceptable, as in Euroseas Group Finance Co. Ltd.

Once the name has been accepted and the necessary fees paid, (see page 11) the company must ensure that its name is mentioned in legible characters outside all company offices and places of business, in all business letters, cheques, bills of exchange, orders, invoices, receipts and notices of the company (C.A. 1985, s.348 and 349). These rules ensure adequate publicity of the corporate name, and if they are not complied with, then any company officer who is responsible may be fined and may be personally liable on the document. This liability could be significant, if for example, the company failed to honour a cheque drawn on its account when the company name was not clearly stated on the cheque (*Durham Fancy Goods Ltd* v. *Michael Jackson (Fancy Goods) Ltd 1968*, where 'Michael Jackson' was abbreviated to 'M. Jackson' and this was held to be in breach of the statutory provisions).

A limited company may change its name by passing a special resolution of the company (C.A. 1985, s.28 and see page 67). The new name is subject to the same restrictions as the old name and must be acceptable to the Registrar. Additionally the Secretary of State may require a company to change its name if the name is the same as or is too like a company name which is already on the Index of Names at Companies House, or if the company name 'gives so misleading an indication of the nature of its activities as to be likely to cause harm to the public' (C.A. 1985, s.32). It would not be difficult to imagine the public confusion if a company running a small pig-breeding farm in a remote part of England had the name 'Global Finance Co. Ltd'.

2 *The situation of the company's registered office*. This may be specified as being in England and Wales, or Wales or Scotland. Every limited company must have a registered office to which all notices and communications may be sent (C.A. 1985, s.287) and any document may be validly served on a company by sending it to the registered office.

A certain amount of company information has to be kept for inspection at the registered office, including: the register of company directors and secretary (C.A. 1985, s.325); details of any charges on company property – that is when the company has, for example, created a mortgage on its property as security for borrowing money from a creditor (C.A. 1985, s.407); minutes of proceedings at any Annual General Meeting (A.G.M.) of the company (C.A. 1985, s.383). Some of this information can be inspected by any person including members of the public whereas some may be inspected only by company shareholders and creditors.

A company can only change the situation of its registered office from one place in the country specified to another within that same country. Its address cannot be changed from one country to another. Any change in the actual address within the country must be notified to the Registrar within fourteen days of the change. In practice, many companies choose to use the company accountants or solicitors as the address of the registered office so that the professional advisers can deal with any official notices. Naturally, the advisers will charge a fee for providing such a service.

3 *The Objects Clause.* The objects clause specifies the company's principal activities – the objects or purposes for which the company was incorporated. It gives information to shareholders and creditors, both existing and potential, as to the nature of the company's business and its contractual powers. A company cannot have illegal objects.

If a company engages in an activity or enters into a contract outside the scope of its objects, this is described as 'ultra vires' – that is, outside the powers of the company. Prior to the European Communities Act 1972, neither the company nor the other party could rely or sue on an 'ultra vires' contract because outsiders dealing with the company were deemed to know the contents of the company's public documents. This was the doctrine of 'constructive' notice. Thus outsiders were deemed to know the objects of the company even if they had not actually read the Memorandum. Even all the shareholders voting together cannot ratify an 'ultra vires' contract (*Re Jon Beauforte Ltd 1953*). Instead, the shareholders would have to vote to change the company's objects to cover the activity in question and then the company could enter into a new contract (see page 17).

To minimise the often harsh effects of the doctrine of 'ultra vires', companies began to draft long lists of objects hoping to cover all activities which they might want to pursue and to add an 'independent objects clause' as the final clause – to the effect that all the specified objects are main objects and are independent of each other and are not restricted by reference to each other (*Cotman* v. *Brougham 1918*). This is still current practice.

The European Communities Act 1972 (now C.A. 1985, s.35) has abolished the doctrine of constructive notice, for outsiders dealing with the company where the company has acted 'ultra vires' its objects. Provided that there is a transaction decided upon by the directors of the company, then the outsider can rely on that contract if he is acting in good faith. The outsider is presumed to be acting in good faith unless there is evidence to the contrary – for example, if the outsider actually knew the contents of the company's objects (*International Sales and Agencies Ltd* v. *Marcus 1982*).

If the outsider can rely on C.A. 1985, s.35 then he can sue the company on the 'ultra vires' contract but s.35 does not operate to enable the company, which has acted 'ultra vires' its own objects, to sue the outsider.

Practically, the issue of 'ultra vires' contracts may never be raised if both the company and the other party perform their respective sides of the contract but if, for example, a company goes into liquidation, the liquidator may seek to recover company funds or property which passed to another party on a contract which was 'ultra vires' the company (*T.C.B. Ltd* v. *Gray 1986*).

Most companies are incorporated to pursue commercial objects and to make a profit but a company may decide to make a 'gift' of some of its funds or property, say to make a charitable donation or subscription. In earlier cases the courts viewed such 'gifts' as 'ultra vires' the company unless they were made in good faith and for the company's benefit and were incidental to the company's main objects. This was often difficult to establish. The contradiction would be obvious where a fur trading company wanted to make a donation to an animal rights campaign!

Recent decisions indicate that if a company has included an express clause in its objects enabling it to make such benevolent, charitable and philanthropic payments, then the company will be deemed to be acting 'intra vires' its objects, (within its powers) if it does so (Re: *Horsley and Weight Ltd 1980*; *Charterbridge Corporation Ltd* v. *Lloyds Bank Ltd 1970*; *Rolled Steel Products Ltd* v. *B.S.C. 1985*). However, a company must not disguise the true nature of such 'gifts', as in *Re Halt Garage Ltd 1978*, where a company paid so-called 'remuneration' to a director of the company who had not worked for the company for several years. Such a 'gift' of the company funds was held to be 'ultra vires' the objects. It should be noted that even if the company has the legal capacity to make such 'gifts' of its property, the company officer who authorised the payment may have exceeded his personal authority and so may be in breach of the duty which he owes to his company (see chapter 3).

A company may change its objects by special resolution of the company (see page 67) for any one of seven stated reasons (C.A. 1985, s.4), for example, to carry on the business more economically and efficiently or to enlarge the local area of operations. If a company alters its objects for one of the stated reasons, any company shareholder holding not less than fifteen per cent in nominal value of the company's issued shares may apply to the court to have the alteration cancelled (C.A. 1985, s.5).

This is a special provision which affords some protection for minority shareholders who do not agree with the majority vote. The court then has an absolute discretion to confirm, vary or deny the alteration to the objects. However, if all the shareholders in the company agree to alter the objects clause, the company can change its objects without going through the s.4 procedure.

4 *A Statement that Liability is Lin.ited.* The Memorandum of a limited company must include a statement to this effect. Consequently, if the shareholders in the company have paid at least the full nominal value for their shares, they cannot be held personally liable for the company's debts.

5 *The Share Capital Clause.* If the limited company has a share capital then the amount of that authorised share capital must be stated together with the type and nominal value of each share – for example – 'the company's share capital is £100 divided into 100 ordinary shares of £1 each'. A limited company may issue shares only up to the amount of its authorised capital as stated in this clause. However, a company may change the clause so as to increase or reduce its authorised share capital (C.A. 1985, s.121 and s.135) and any such change must be notified to the Registrar (see page 35). Where a businessman has purchased an 'off the shelf' company, the company formation agents are likely to have formed the company with authorised share capital of £100 (often known as the '£100 private limited company'). This amount may subsequently prove inadequate for the business and the company would need to increase the figure to enable it to issue additional shares.

4 *Articles of Association*

The Articles of Association set out the internal rules which will affect the way in which the company will be run. The Articles cover such matters as: the appointment, remuneration and retirement of directors and auditors; notice and procedures for company meetings and board meetings; rights of shareholders. Table A, set out in the Schedule to the Companies Act 1985, is a model set of Articles but the businessman should ensure that the Articles which are registered for his particular company accurately reflect any specific requirements he may have for that company. In particular, the directors of the company may wish to include in the Articles a clause giving them an absolute discretion to refuse to register a proposed share transfer. If such a clause were included and the directors exercised this power, they would have considerable influence on the future ownership of shares in the company – a matter which could be of significance in a small private company.

It may also be prudent for the Articles of a small private company to include a clause giving existing shareholders priority rights to buy the shares of any other shareholder wishing to sell. This is known as a 'pre-emption clause' and has the effect of preventing an existing shareholder transferring his shares to a non-member who might not be favoured by the other existing shareholders. The existing shareholders effectively have the 'first bite of the cherry' and in that way can ensure that the company's shares remain in the hands of a particular group of shareholders and their approved successors.

Every limited company has the inalienable right to change its Articles by passing a special resolution of the company (C.A. 1985, s.9). The Registrar must be informed of any such resolution. However, if every one of the shareholders agree to alter the Articles, then the alteration will be effective even if the s.9 procedure is not used (*Cane* v. *Jones 1979*). A valid alteration to the Articles will be as binding as any original clause in the Articles.

There are, however, certain restrictions on the power

to alter the Articles of a limited company and it should be noted that provisions in the Memorandum are always dominant over provisions in the Articles, so that if the Memorandum contains a clause which conflicts with a regulation in the Articles, then effectively the regulation in the Articles will be ignored (*Re Duncan Gilmour & Co. Ltd 1952*). Further, section 9 cannot be used to alter the Articles to cause a variation of any special class rights attaching to a particular group of shares (see page 24). In any case, any proposed alteration to the Articles must be made in good faith in the interests of the company as a whole. In *Sidebottom* v. *Kershaw Leese & Co. Ltd 1920*, the court permitted an alteration to the Articles which would have allowed the directors to require any member who competed with the company's business to transfer his shares at full value to the directors' nominees. Such an alteration was found to be for the benefit of the company. Presumably, it was in the company's best interests that a shareholder should not be able to attend the company meetings, learn of the company's business and then go away with better knowledge as to how to compete with the company!

5 Contractual Effect of the Memorandum and Articles

The effect of s.14, C.A. 1985, is to make the provisions in the Memorandum and Articles the basis of the contractual relationship between the company and the shareholders. The investor advances his money for shares in the company on the basis of the terms and conditions in the Memorandum and Articles, which he is bound to accept and which the company is bound to observe.

2 Shares and Capital

The limited company will issue shares in order to raise finance for the business. The expanding and developing company may especially need to raise such share capital. People who invest in the company will become shareholders and their investment becomes the share capital of the company. The power to issue company shares will normally be exercised by the company directors (see page 49) but it should be noted that a company can only issue shares up to the amount of its authorised or nominal share capital. This figure will be clearly stated in the Memorandum of the company and this same clause will also state the amount that each share is divided into – that is, the par or nominal value of each share (see page 18). If a company has already issued shares up to the total amount of its authorised share capital, that figure must first be increased according to the proper procedure, before the company can issue any further shares. Suppose, for example, the authorised share capital of a company is £100, divided into 100 shares of £1 each and the company has already allotted all the 100 shares to various shareholders in exchange for cash. If the company wishes to issue additional shares to raise more cash, it must first increase the amount of its authorised share capital – say from the stated £100 to £1,000. The company can then issue an additional 900 shares of £1 each.

In many smaller private companies, those who run the business will often hold the majority of the shares

in the company and may also be named as the directors
of the company.

1 Definition of a Share

Although the terms shareholder and member are often
taken to mean the same thing, strictly, it is possible for
a person to be a shareholder in a company and not
necessarily also to be a member of that company. A
person may buy shares in a company and sell those
shares within a few days. For that short period, he is
a shareholder in the company but he is not a member
of that company unless and until his name is entered
on the company's Register of Members (see page 25).
Practically, however, in most private companies the
shareholders will be registered members.

In *Borland's Trustee* v. *Steel Bros Co. Ltd 1901*, a share
was said to represent the interest of the shareholder in
the company. The share is measured by a sum of money
for the purpose of liability and interest.

The shareholder has an interest in the company as
a total business undertaking. He has no claim over
individual items of company property.

Further, every share issued by a company must have
a stated nominal or par value. In the case of a private
company purchased 'off the shelf', the par value of the
shares is usually £1. Even though the actual value of
the shares may fluctuate from time to time, the par
value is not affected by the changing fortunes of the
company. In the rare case where a private company
declares a dividend on its shares, the dividend is
declared and calculated as a percentage of the par value
of the shares irrespective of the real value of the shares –
for example, a ten per cent dividend on shares with a
par value of £1 is ten pence per share. Most Public
Limited Companies do declare dividends on their

shares and so it is important for the investing share-holder to know what is the par value of his shares. Companies incorporated in the United Kingdom cannot issue shares of no par or nominal value.

If at least the full nominal value of the shares has been paid to the company, then the shares are described as fully-paid and no further liability attaches to the holder of the shares. So even if the shares are transferred to another person at a later date, the company cannot claim any additional payment from him. Even if the company is wound up owing considerable amounts of money, the shareholder who holds fully paid shares in the company cannot be held personally liable for the company's debts. Alternatively, if the company is wound up and having paid all its debts, considerable assets remain, these assets will be divided among the company shareholders in proportion to the number of shares that each holds.

2 Different Types of Shares

Depending on its particular structure and requirements, a company may issue several different types of shares.

1 Ordinary Shares

The ordinary share is by far the most common type of share. The holder of ordinary shares takes the full risks and the full profits of the business. The ordinary share usually carries full voting rights – say, one vote for every ordinary share held. The holder of ordinary shares in a company is entitled to notice of all company meetings and is entitled to attend and vote at such meetings. In this way, the ordinary shareholder can directly influence the way in which the company is run. Although the directors will usually have general powers of management of the company, the Companies Act 1985 requires that certain important matters must be voted on by the company in general meeting. For these purposes, the company *is* the voting shareholders (and see Chapter 3). It follows therefore that a person who holds a large number of the ordinary shares in a company may significantly affect the running of the company.

2 Preference Shares

Some older established companies may have issued preference shares. Generally preference shares were issued to raise capital for the company's use without necessarily affecting the balance of voting power within the company. Preference shares usually have very restricted voting rights – for example, the Articles may state that the preference shareholders can only vote on matters which directly affect their position. As the name implies, the preference share will carry some kind of preference – usually relating to dividend or capital rights. For example, if a company issues '1,000 six per cent £1 preference shares', the holders of those shares will be entitled to receive a preferential dividend of six per cent on every £1 share *before* the ordinary shareholders receive any dividend at all. Any preferential class rights which attach to preference shares are usually clearly stated in the Articles of the company.

It is unusual for modern companies to issue preference shares because a company needing to raise medium or long-term finance will prefer to borrow the money from, for example, a bank (see Chapter 5). Although the company will usually be required to give some security for the borrowing to the lender, nevertheless the lender remains merely a creditor of the company – not a member of the company. As a creditor, the lender is not entitled to attend or vote at company meetings and so cannot directly interfere with the running of the company.

In the unlikely event that the private company has issued a special class of preference shares, the company must comply with the procedure in section 125, Companies Act 1985, if it wishes to vary or change those class rights.

3 Employees' Shares

Companies are being encouraged to create a special class of shares which are issued directly to the employees of the company or which are held by trustees on behalf of the employees. In this way the employees will have a 'stake' in the company in which they work and if profits are good, the employees will get the benefit of a dividend on the shares.

3 Register of Members

Every limited company must keep a Register of its members. The Register should state the name and address of, and the number of shares held by, each member. The date on which a person becomes or ceases to be a registered member should also be entered on the Register (C.A. 1985, s.352). If there are more than fifty members, the company is required to keep an index of their names. The Register can be inspected by the company members and by the public (C.A. 1985, s.356). As has been noted, the shareholder who is a registered member of a company may attend and vote at company meetings (see page 23). A company is entitled to treat a registered member as the legal and beneficial owner of the shares. If a member's name is omitted from or wrongly included in the Register the

court can order that the Register should be rectified
(C.A. 1985, s.359).

The company's Annual Return must also give details
of the company members (see page 71).

4 Payment for Shares

A contract for the issue and allotment of shares is, like
any other contract, based on offer and acceptance. In
most private companies, the shareholder will pay at
least the full par or nominal value for the shares and
in exchange the shares will be allotted to him by the
company. If the shareholder is required to pay more
than the nominal value, this extra amount is known as
the share premium – for example, if the company
requires the shareholder to pay £1.25 for every £1
share – the share premium on each share is twenty-five
pence.

A company cannot issue shares at less than their
nominal value. Shares cannot be issued at a discount.
However, shares can be issued as 'partly-paid'. If the
nominal value of the shares is £1 the company may
require the shareholder to pay only seventy-five pence
immediately but the company will 'call' for the
outstanding twenty-five pence on each share at some
time in the future. When the company receives the final
twenty-five pence the issued shares then become 'fully
paid'.

Private companies can allot shares in exchange for
money or 'money's worth'. The term 'money's worth'
includes good-will and 'know how', as well as more
tangible items such as buildings and equipment (C.A.
1985, s.99). It is not uncommon for a private company
to be formed specifically to acquire the existing business
of a sole trader or partnership. Shares in the newly
formed company will then be allotted to the vendor of

the business in exchange for which the business assets, including good-will, will be transferred to the company. In such cases, professional advice should always be sought to ensure that the transfer is not deemed to be a disposal of assets which may give rise to a charge to Capital Gains Tax.

The private limited company has virtually unlimited freedom to accept any kind of consideration in return for an allotment of its shares. The courts will only intervene in cases of fraud.

If a company has alloted its shares and has received payment in full, then the price at which those shares may be subsequently transferred is a matter only for the buyer and seller of the shares.

5 Share Certificate

When a company receives payment for and allots its shares, the member's name is entered on the Register and the company issues a share certificate to that member. The member's name and the number of shares he holds are stated on the certificate. The share certificate is 'prima facie' evidence that the person named on the certificate is the owner of the shares. The share certificate should be issued within two months of the allotment of the shares (C.A. 1985, s.185).

6 Share Transfers

The basic rule is that all shares are freely transferable but it should be remembered that the Articles of most private companies will contain some restrictions on the transfer of their shares (see page 19).

The Articles may contain a 'pre-emption' clause

which gives existing company members priority rights to buy the shares of any other member wishing to sell. This standard provision restricts the freedom of members to transfer their shares and enables the founding members of a private company to maintain tight control over the company's shares. The Court of Appeal recently decided in *Tett* v. *Phoenix Property and Investment Co. Ltd, 1985*, that any transfer of shares made in breach of a 'pre-emption' provision in the company's Articles, was not a valid transfer. A 'pre-emption' clause is a valid and enforceable condition which must be complied with. Only if there are no other existing members who wish to buy the shares, will the selling shareholder have the right to transfer his shares to a non-member of the company.

The Articles may also give the company directors an absolute discretion to refuse to register a proposed share transfer. This is a fiduciary power and should always be exercised in good faith and in the interests of the company as a whole (and see chapter 3). However, it is very difficult to establish that the directors have exercised this discretion for the wrong reasons if they do not give a reason for refusing to register any particular share transfer. In any case, the directors' discretion must be exercised within a reasonable period. Under section 183, Companies Act 1985 and following the decision in *Re Swaledale Cleaners Ltd, 1968*, the reasonable period is two months from the date that the transfer is presented.

If all the provisions in the company's Articles are complied with, the vendor of the shares should complete the necessary Stock Transfer Form in favour of the purchaser. The purchaser then pays the small amount of Stamp Duty on the transfer and submits it usually to the company Secretary for registration. The Secretary will enter the name of the new member on the membership Register, cancel the old certificate and issue a new share certificate (within two months) in the purchaser's name. Naturally, if the directors and Secretary know that a 'pre-emption' clause in the Articles has not been complied with, they should not register a transfer of the shares.

7 The Company as a Member of Itself

Significant changes in the law were introduced in 1981 which made it possible for a limited company to buy its own shares at any time provided it is authorised to do so by its Articles.

These provisions may be especially useful in the case of a private company with only a few 'family' shareholders. An existing member may wish to sell his shares or, if the member has died, his executors may wish to sell but the remaining members, whilst wishing to keep the shares within the 'family' control, cannot afford to buy. In this instance, if the company itself has funds, the company can purchase the shares thereby preventing the shares from leaving the 'family' control. The company is using its own money for the purchase of its own shares (C.A. 1985, s.162) and effectively becomes a member of itself!

The purchase money must be found from either the accumulated profits of the company, which would otherwise be available for distribution as dividend, or from the proceeds of a fresh issue of shares. In the event of a shortfall of funds from these sources, the private company *only* can fund the purchase of its own shares out of its capital assets (C.A. 1985, s.171). It must be stressed, however, that there are clear statutory procedures which must be strictly observed if the private company wishes to use its own capital to buy its own shares. Additionally, the directors of the private company should be aware that they are required to make a statutory declaration as to the company's present and future solvency. If the company is wound up within one year after its capital was used to buy its own shares, the directors involved may be held personally liable to repay to the company any loss of capital which it suffered.

This potential future liability and the reluctance of company directors and auditors to commit themselves to forecasting the company's future solvency may dissuade them from making use of the special statutory powers. The complex procedures now enable the limited company to buy and redeem its own shares but in all cases, the businessman should seek competent professional advice before embarking on such a course. He must not simply write out a company cheque!

8 Providing Financial Assistance for the Purchase of its own Shares

The Companies Act 1985 recasts the restrictions imposed on a company for the purpose of certain share acquisitions.

A limited company is prohibited from giving any financial assistance, either directly or indirectly, for the purpose of an acquisition of shares in the company. The company is prohibited from giving such assistance to any person before or at the time he acquires the company's shares (C.A. 1985, s.151).

The term financial assistance includes any gift, loan, guarantee or indemnity made by the company. If, for example, A Co. Ltd buys from B some goods or commodity which A Co. Ltd genuinely wants to acquire for its own commercial purposes and makes the purchase having no other purpose in view, the fact that B then uses the proceeds of the sale to buy shares in A Co. Ltd would not amount to a breach of the section.

However, if A Co. Ltd, without regard to its own commercial interests, buys something from B and the sole purpose of the transaction is to put B in funds so that B can buy shares in A Co. Ltd, this would clearly contravene section 151, even if the price paid was a fair price for what was bought by A Co. Ltd – *Belmont Finance Corpn Ltd* v. *Williams Furniture Ltd, 1980*. In the second situation, A Co. Ltd has clearly provided financial assistance to enable B to buy shares in A Co. Ltd.

If there are two or more purposes behind the giving of the financial assistance by a company there is no infringement of section 151, if the *principal* purpose is *not* to give financial assistance for the purchase of its own shares. If the giving of the assistance is merely incidental to a larger genuinely commercial purpose, this will not fall foul of the section.

Certain company actions are specifically excluded from the scope of the prohibition – for example, if the limited company lawfully declares a dividend on its shares and an existing shareholder then uses that dividend to buy more shares in the company, there is no breach of section 151.

Despite the basic prohibition, the Companies Act 1985 sets out a procedure which will enable a private company *only* to provide financial assistance to another person for the purpose of enabling that person to buy shares in the company. The procedure is almost identical to that which must be followed if the private company wants to use its own capital to directly purchase its own shares (see page 29). So, provided certain conditions are satisfied, a private company could lend money to a person which he then uses to buy shares in that same company (C.A. 1985, s.155).

In *Wallersteiner* v. *Moir, 1974*, the Court of Appeal noted that transactions infringing what is now section 151 can be very complex and may be disguised by misleading entries in the company's books. It is necessary to ignore the masquerades and look to the realities of the transactions. As Lord Denning said: 'You look to the company's money and see what has become of it. You look to the company's shares and see into whose hands they have got. You will then soon see if the company's money has been used to finance the purchase.'

The company itself is liable to a fine for a breach of section 151. Every company officer responsible is also liable to a fine and imprisonment but perhaps the most effective sanction is that as the whole transaction is illegal, it is therefore regarded as void and of no effect. The illegal transaction cannot be relied upon or sued upon by any of the parties involved in it (*Heald* v. *O'Connor, 1971*).

To allow even a private company to use its own resources to provide financial assistance for the purchase of its own shares by others, without imposing strict controls, would be to allow an unauthorised reduction of the company's capital (see page 36). The position of the creditors and the shareholders of the company could be seriously jeopardised.

9 The Majority versus the Minority

All powers in a company rest either with the shareholders in general meeting of the company or with the Board of Directors (see pages 61 and 66). On many occasions the courts have expressed their unwillingness to interfere in the running of a company as a commercial enterprise, unless for example, there is evidence of fraud (see page 86).

The time honoured and democratic principle of majority rule means that the minority shareholders must accept the decisions of the majority but in some cases, an aggrieved minority shareholder may be prejudiced by the acts of the majority. Say, for instance, the Articles of a private company restrict a shareholder's right to freely transfer his shares (see page 19). The minority shareholder may find that he cannot sell his shares and is therefore prevented from withdrawing his investment in the company. This hardly seems fair.

The Companies Act of 1980 provided a new remedy, particularly for minority shareholders. This remedy is now to be found in section 459, Companies Act, 1985. The aggrieved shareholder can petition the court and ask the court to grant relief if his interests are being unfairly prejudiced by the way in which the company's affairs are being conducted. It is the way in which the courts are now interpreting the phrase 'unfairly prejudicial' which will be of special interest to the small shareholder. In *Re Bovey Hotel Ventures Ltd, 1981*, Mr Justice Slade said:

A member of a company will be able to bring himself within the section if he can show that the value of his shareholding in the company has been seriously diminished or at least seriously jeopardised by reason of a course of conduct on the part of those persons who have (effective) control of the company, which has been unfair to the member concerned. . . . The test is, whether a reasonable bystander observing the consequences of their (the controllers') conduct would regard it as having unfairly prejudiced the (members') interests.

So if, say, the directors and majority shareholders consistently failed to send out notices of company meetings or even failed to hold any company meetings or failed to count the votes of a shareholder at a company meeting, the shareholder should ask the court for a remedy under section 459 (*Re Garage Door Associates Ltd, 1984*).

It is doubtful, however, that a minority shareholder could establish that he was being unfairly prejudiced if the directors declined to recommend the declaration of a dividend on the company shares, provided that the directors were acting in good faith and in the company's interests – as where the profits were being retained for the future development of the company (cf *Re R A Noble & Sons Ltd, 1983*).

However, if the court is satisfied that the shareholder is being unfairly prejudiced, the court can make any order it thinks fit in order to give relief in respect of the matters complained of (C.A. 1985, s.461). Specifically, the court can order that the shares of the member whose interests are being prejudiced, should be purchased by the other members. The court would order the majority to 'buy out' the minority shareholder. The purchase price will be determined by the court and in *Re Bird Precision Bellows Ltd, 1984*, the court had to consider the issue of a valuation of shares in such a case. Mr Justice Norse said,

> On the assumption that the unfair prejudice has made it no longer tolerable for (the minority shareholder) to retain his interest in the company, a sale of his shares will invariably be his only practical way out, short of a winding up. In that kind of case it seems to me that it would not merely be not fair but most unfair that he should be bought out . . . on any basis which involved a discounted price, and the correct course would be to fix the price pro rata according to the value of the shares as a whole and without any discount.

The aggrieved member should receive a fair price for his shares and such a remedy, at least, enables him to withdraw his investment in the company and to take it elsewhere.

A petition for a remedy under section 459 does not

preclude any action which the minority shareholder might also be able to take under the 'fraud on the minority' exception to the Rule in *Foss* v. *Harbottle* or under the 'just and equitable' winding up principles (see pages 54 and 85).

10 Increase of Capital

The businessman who buys an 'off the shelf' company will usually find that it is incorporated with an authorised share capital of £100 – the "£100 private company" (see page 18). If however, he is incorporating the company to his own specific requirements, the businessman should bear in mind the possible future capital needs of the company and should fix the authorised share capital clause accordingly.

If, during its lifetime, the company wishes and needs to raise additional finance, say for expansion and development, the company may decide to issue more shares. However, as has been noted, if the company has already issued shares up to the full amount of its authorised capital, the company will first have to increase that authorised capital figure before it can proceed to allot the newly-created additional shares (see page 26).

Provided it has the necessary power in its Articles (ART. 32), a limited company can increase the amount of its authorised share capital. The proposed increase must be approved by an ordinary resolution of the company members in a general meeting (C.A. 1985, s.121 and see page 67). A copy of the resolution must be sent to the Registrar within fifteen days (C.A. 1985, s.123). Additionally, since any increase in the amount of a company's authorised capital will result in a change to the share capital clause in the Memorandum (see page 21), a copy of the Memorandum, as altered, must also be sent to the Registrar. The Registrar will then notify official receipt of the copy in the London Gazette.

When the necessary formalities are completed, the company can then proceed to allot the additional shares (see page 26).

11 Reduction of Capital

Provided it has the necessary power in its Articles (ART. 34), a limited company can reduce the amount of its issued share capital. The issued capital represents the capital raised by the company from its shareholders in return for the allotment of its shares. The reduction must be approved by a special resolution of the company members in a general meeting and, most importantly, must then be confirmed by the court (C.A. 1985, s.135).

A reduction of capital may take any form but section 135 refers specifically to three of the most usual situations –

1 where the company is eliminating or reducing liability on shares in respect of capital not paid up;
2 where the company is cancelling 'lost' paid up capital;
3 where the company is returning paid up capital which is in excess of its requirements.

Method 1 might be desirable where a company's original capital has been raised by issuing partly-paid shares (see page 26) and contrary to original estimates, further capital is not required. Under this method, the company would cut (or reduce) the nominal or par value of each issued share so that it then becomes fully paid. For example, if the company has issued £1 shares which are originally partly-paid at fifty pence, and if the par value is then reduced to fifty pence per share, they become fully paid fifty pence shares. The company does not actually lose any current existing capital but forgoes the right to call for that extra capital at some stage in the future.

Method 2 is used where a company has suffered a series of trading losses and the balance sheet discloses a cumulative adverse balance on the profit and loss account. The purpose of the reduction of capital in such a case is to bring the amount of issued capital more realistically into line with the value of the assets by which it is represented. It also creates a balance sheet presentation which should have the effect of restoring confidence in the company. This method does not involve the company's assets being returned to the shareholders.

Method 3 could be used where a company has sold part of its business, with a view to curtailing its activities, but has thereby received cash which it cannot usefully employ. If the company returns this cash to the shareholders it reduces its capital to reasonable proportions. This way the company avoids the necessity of paying large dividends on top-heavy capital, much of which can no longer be gainfully employed.

Clearly, a reduction of capital may prejudice the position of certain people with an interest in the company. When it is considering whether or not to confirm a reduction of capital, the court will take account of:

- the interests of the creditors of the company;
- whether any different classes of shareholders are treated fairly and equitably;
- whether the interests of the public, as potential investors and creditors in the company, are best served.

1 Interests of Creditors

If the proposed reduction is under method (a) or (c) above, or if the court so directs in any case, the creditors of the company are entitled to object to the reduction (C.A. 1985, s.136). However, it is well established that a creditor cannot oppose the reduction if there is no evidence of the company's assets being returned to the shareholders – *Re Meux's Brewery Co. Ltd 1919*. If a creditor can and does object to the reduction, a list of the company's creditors must be drawn up stating the nature and amount of their claims. The company must then either pay them all or, if the debt is reasonably disputed, make a payment into court to secure the debt. This can obviously be an expensive and time-consuming exercise and the court has the power to dispense with the list of creditors if it is satisfied that the company has made adequate provision for satisfying the legitimate claims of the creditors. In *Re Grosvenor Press P.L.C., 1985*, the court dispensed with the list of creditors on receiving an undertaking from the company that all the existing creditors would be paid in full.

2 Interests of Shareholders

If the company has issued shares of different types, the court will be concerned to ensure that the reduction is fair and equitable to each class of shareholder (and see page 23). A reduction of capital may be used to repay a whole class of shareholders, thereby eliminating them but even this will be held to be fair and equitable provided there is no variation of their special class rights. For example, if the company reduces capital and pays off a class of preference shareholders, they cannot claim that they are being unfairly treated simply because they lose the opportunity to enjoy a fixed preferential dividend – *Prudential Assurance Co. Ltd* v. *Chatterley-Whitfield Collieries Ltd, 1949*. A company must be generally free to change its capital structure.

3 Interests of the Public

The reduction must not result in the confusion of or be misleading to people who may deal with the company in the future. After the company has passed the special resolution to reduce its issued capital, the court has the discretion to confirm, vary or disallow the reduction. If the court makes an order confirming the reduction, a copy of the court order and a note of the new details of the company's share capital must be lodged with the Registrar.

This very formal procedure for a reduction of a company's capital applies to all those figures in the company's accounts which are treated as capital, including share premiums (see page 26). It is not, however, applicable if the company uses its own capital to buy its own shares or where it redeems its own shares, when different procedures must be followed (see page 29).

3   Directors and Secretary

1 Appointment of Directors

Every private limited company must have at least one director who must not also be the company secretary. The director need not necessarily be a shareholder in the company although in many small companies the majority shareholders will also be the company directors. (Every P.L.C. must have at least two directors.) However, the fact that a director is also a shareholder does not limit his responsibility as a director. The distinction between the two capacities is crucial.

Although it is not uncommon for a person who holds a large number of the shares in a company to be named also as a director and yet take little or no part in the day to day running of the business, in many cases the director will also be a full-time employee of the company. He is known as an 'executive' director. Some large companies may also appoint 'non-executive' directors who are not full-time employees of the company but, rather, act as advisers to the full-time executive directors.

In certain circumstances a particular person may be regarded as a 'shadow' director because although not specifically named as a director of the company, he gives instructions to the actual directors as to how the company should be run. Effectively therefore, the 'shadow' director is acting as if he were a properly appointed director and the law will treat him as such and will impose on him the duties and responsibilities of a director.

The director is an officer of the company who is entrusted with the management of the company. The Articles of most modern companies provide that the business of the company is the responsibility of the Board of Directors and that the company, through the votes of its shareholders, will control the appointment of the directors. When a person is appointed as a director he must file with the Registrar, on the appropriate form, his written consent to act as a director. Generally directors are appointed at the A.G.M. of the company (see Chapter 4) although the Articles usually provide that the Board itself may appoint additional directors at other times and it is then for the shareholders at the subsequent A.G.M. to decide whether or not to confirm the Board's choice. If the shareholders are also the directors, this should not be a problem! The model set of Articles in Table A state that at the company's first A.G.M. all the directors should retire from office and at every subsequent A.G.M. one third should retire by rotation (ART. 73). If there are less than three directors, the number nearest to one third shall retire.

Where a director retires by rotation, then unless somebody is elected in his place, that director is automatically re-elected so long as he offers (ART. 75). Naturally there would be no automatic re-election if the company voted positively not to re-elect him. A private company can appoint one or more directors by a single resolution of the company whereas each director of a P.L.C. must be appointed by a separate resolution.

2 Who Can Be A Director?

The general rule is that any adult person may be appointed as a director of a private company. However, the aspiring director should note that there are some important legal prohibitions on the appointment of certain people as directors. In recent years the number of directors, in both public and private companies, who have apparently abused their position has increased and Parliament has introduced two new highly significant pieces of legislation: The Company Directors Disqualification Act 1986 and The Insolvency Act 1986. This new legislation will have a dramatic effect on the company director and on the professionals who advise him. The director has never been more vulnerable to disqualification and potential personal liability (and see chapter 6).

A person cannot be appointed as a director if he is an undischarged bankrupt, unless the court permits (C.D.D.A. 1986, s.11). The court may disqualify a person from holding office as a director if he is convicted of a serious criminal offence in connection with the formation, management or liquidation of a limited company. This disqualification can be for a period of up to fifteen years! (C.D.D.A. 1986, s.2.). Further, a person may be disqualified from being a director for up to five years if it appears that he has been persistently in default in making the necessary company returns or filing the necessary company documents with the Registrar (C.D.D.A. 1986, s.3, and see chapter 4). The small company director may be so involved in the daily running of the business that he overlooks the filing requirements of the Companies Act 1985. Perhaps it would be advisable to entrust such necessary paperwork to professional advisers, like the company accountant or solicitor.

The Insolvency Act 1986 empowers the courts to make far-reaching orders against directors of insolvent companies. They can disqualify a person from being a director and make him personally liable for his conduct and order him to make some contribution to the company's assets (see Chapter 6).

Theoretically the courts' power to make a disqualification order is important as it can be used to reduce fraud and mismanagement in limited companies. In practice however, it should be noted that the courts' power is discretionary and any proceedings against the director, if brought at all, may well arise several years after the incident in question. It is, of course, possible that in the light of the recent abuses, the investigation procedure will be speeded up and that many more cases will come before the courts.

3 The Director as an Employee of the Company

For the purposes of Company Law and Employment Law, it is important to determine whether a particular company director is also an employee of his company. These two roles are quite distinct and the same person may be regarded, on the one hand, as a company director, with all the attendant duties and responsibilities and, on the other, as an employee of the company (see Chapter 15). Effectively such a person is wearing two different hats! Unfortunately it is not always easy to draw a clear dividing line. All properly appointed directors are officers of the company but not all are also employees.

If a director has negotiated a formal service contract or contract of employment with his company, he is regarded as an employee of the company. His rights and duties will therefore depend on the terms and conditions of this contract, including his right to remuneration or payment. In the past some major abuses have occurred when company directors, particularly those who were also majority shareholders, ensured that they had very long term service contracts with their company so that they enjoyed considerable security of employment. Even if they were dismissed

they were able to claim substantial compensation for
breach of contract (see page 230). C.A. 1985, s.319 now
provides a check on the possibility of such abuses. It
prevents a company from entering into a long-term
service contract with a director which the company
cannot terminate by notice, unless the company has
approved the contract in general meeting. If the
contract is for more than five years it is regarded as
being determinable by the company by giving reasonable notice, at any time, to the director in question. If
the company gives reasonable notice of termination,
say between three and six months, then this is effective
to bring the contract to an end and the director is not
entitled to compensation for breach of that contract. It
would be prudent for the small company director to
negotiate a five year service contract in the first instance
and then for such a director, if possible, to protect
himself by renegotiating his contract for a further five
years at each subsequent company A.G.M. Consequently if he were dismissed shortly after an A.G.M.
he could at least claim over four years worth of salary
as compensation for loss of office.

In any case where a director has a written service
contract, the company is required to keep at the appropriate place, usually the Registered Office, a copy of
that contract and if it is not in writing, the company
must keep a written memorandum of the terms of the
agreement (C.A. 1985, s.318.).

A director with a service contract who is regarded as
an employee will enjoy certain rights under his contract
including the right to seek compensation for wrongful
dismissal if he is dismissed without notice or with inadequate notice. Modern employment law protection will
entitle him to a redundancy payment (*Morley* v. *C. T.
Morley Ltd 1985*). Even if the company goes into liquidation (see Chapter 6) with few or no assets, the
company director who is also an employee may be able

to claim a redundancy payment from the Redundancy Fund which is under the control of the Secretary of State. Naturally, the director should ensure that his National Insurance contributions are paid up to date!

Even if a director has not negotiated an *express* service contract with his company, it is possible for the law to *imply* a contract of service (and see Chapter 15). This may be of special relevance in the case of a director of a smaller private company where that director 'devotes his whole time to the affairs of the company; does all in his power to develop and extend the business of the company and does not engage in any other business'. So when considering the possible employment status of a person named as a director, the following points appear to be relevant:

- whether that person is paid and taxed as an employee or is merely paid director's fees. This information will be found in the company accounts (see page 69)
- whether his contributions for National Insurance are as an employed or self-employed person
- whether the company keeps written evidence of a service contract (see page 44)
- whether he works regularly and consistently for the company.

If a service contract can be *implied*, the director is also an employee of the company and is protected by employment law legislation in the same way as a director with an *express* contract (cf *Parsons* v. *Albert J. Parsons & Sons Ltd. 1978*).

In the absence of an express or implied service contract, the director is regarded only as an officer of the company and his rights and duties will depend on the provisions in the Articles of Association.

The businessman should note that it is unlawful for a company to make any tax free payment to its director and any such payments will be treated as subject to tax (C.A. 1985, s.377.). Notwithstanding the legal rules relating to loans to directors (see page 56) the Inland Revenue will consider the lending of money by a company to its director to be a taxable event.

4 Termination of Appointment

Section 303, C.A. 1985 gives every limited company a special inalienable power to remove a director by passing an ordinary resolution at a general meeting of the company (see page 67). Practically, however, if the director is also the majority shareholder, he may not feel inclined to vote to remove himself! The company must give special notice of such a proposal and the director in question is entitled to have his written reply to the proposal circulated to the company shareholders or read out at the meeting.

Section 303 can be used to remove any director at any time, whether he has a service contract with his company or not. However, as already pointed out, such a director is entitled to claim compensation for breach of contract from the company (see page 44).

Any claim by the director would, of course, be subject to a possible counter-claim by the company alleging that the director himself was somehow in breach of the contract – as where the director had spent more time in the local public house than in his office! However, if the company makes a payment to a dismissed director over and above the amount which it is contractually bound to make, the details of such a 'gratuitous' payment must be first disclosed to and approved by the company in general meeting (C.A. 1985, s.312 and *Taupo Totara Timber Co. Ltd* v. *Rowe 1977*). The shareholders are entitled to be told of any 'golden handshakes' which the company proposes to pay to its ex-directors.

The appointment of a director may also be terminated under certain provisions in the company's Articles – for example, if the Articles provide that a person shall cease to be a director if he resigns, or becomes of unsound mind, or is absent without leave for more than six consecutive months (ART. 81, Table A). It might be wise for a private company to ensure that such a provision *was* included in its Articles. The private company director might be relieved to learn that he is not required, by law, to retire at seventy years of age, whereas the director of a P.L.C. should normally retire at seventy! (C.A. 1985, s.293.).

5 The Position of the Director in Law

The company director is a kind of legal 'hybrid'. In some situations the director is viewed as being in the position of a trustee because he is responsible for looking after the assets of the company and must exercise his powers in good faith and for the benefit of the company as a whole. The director owes a fiduciary duty to his company and he must not allow his personal interests to conflict with his duty to the company. So, for example, if a director wrongly authorises the sale of company property to a personal friend at a price which is below the market value, he will be in breach of his fiduciary duty. If the director uses company money to fund an item of his own personal expenditure, he will be in breach of his duty to his company and will be personally liable to repay the money.

In other situations the director is more like an agent of the company. For example, where the director is acting within the scope of his authority and he negotiates and signs a contract on behalf of his company.

The company is the principal and the director is the agent and represents his company to outsiders. The director can legally bind his company on such a contract. Conversely, if a director signs a contract with an outsider, without revealing that he is acting as an agent for his company, he may be held personally liable on the contract (see Chapter 7).

In yet other situations the director is regarded as an employee of his company (see page 43).

The company director wears many 'hats' and it is impossible to describe the duties of a director simply by way of analogy with persons acting in other capacities.

6 Duties of a Director

The duties of a director derive mainly from three sources – namely:

- Fiduciary duties
- Duties of care and skill
- Statutory duties.

In recent years Parliament (through the Companies Acts and other legislation) has considerably increased the statutory duties imposed on directors of limited companies and in several areas the statutory duties were introduced to reinforce the older fiduciary duties and duties of care and skill.

1 Fiduciary Duties

As a fiduciary, the director must act in good faith for the benefit of the company as a whole. He must not use his position as a director to benefit himself at the expense of his company (*Re Smith and Fawcett Ltd. 1942*) It should be emphasised that the director owes his fiduciary duty to the company as a whole, as a separate legal entity, and that the duty is not generally owed to individual shareholders or creditors or employees of the company (*Percival* v. *Wright 1902*). It follows that if a director is in breach of his fiduciary duty to his company then the company can bring an action against the director. The company will bring the action in its corporate name, as a distinct legal entity (*Foss* v. *Harbottle 1843*, and see page 54). It may be helpful to identify several different situations which may arise during the 'life' of a company when the director is required to exercise his powers in good faith for the benefit of the company as a whole.

1 Issuing Unissued Shares. A director may not exercise any power of his company to allot unissued shares unless he has been given specific authority to do so either by an ordinary resolution of the company in general meeting or by the Articles (C.A. 1985, s.80). Even if the director does have this specific authority, any allotment of the company's unissued shares (see page 21) must be made in good faith for the benefit of the company. If, for example, the company genuinely needed to raise additional cash for expansion, it would be proper for the director to issue any unissued shares to raise the necessary finance (*Howard Smith Ltd* v. *Ampol Petroleum Ltd 1974*). However, it has been held by the courts that where the primary purpose for issuing shares was to block a take-over of the company or to dilute the voting strength of an existing shareholder, then the allotment was not for a 'proper purpose' and therefore not in the best interests of the company (see *Hogg* v. *Cramphorn Ltd 1967* and *Clemens* v. *Clemens Bros Ltd 1976*). The courts will set aside any share allotment which they feel is not made 'bona fide' – that is, in good faith – and in the company's interests as a whole. In practice, it should be possible for company directors to disclose to the shareholders in a general meeting, the purpose of any proposed share issue – even a so-called 'improper' purpose – and if at that meeting the shareholders approve the issue, then it can hardly be said subsequently to be *not* in the interests of the company as a whole (*Bamford* v. *Bamford 1970*).

2 *Secret Profit*. A director must not use his position to make a secret profit for himself. As a fiduciary, the director is under a duty to account to his company for any profit he makes out of his position. He must disclose the full amount of any such profit to the company in general meeting (*Regal (Hastings) Ltd* v. *Gulliver 1942*). Naturally, if the director were also the majority shareholder he could vote in favour of himself retaining that profit, providing there was no evidence of 'equitable fraud' (see page 55). So, for example, a director must reveal to his company full details of any commissions he receives on any company contracts because he has been paid the commissions by virtue of being a director involved in the contracts. If a company director were allowed to use his position to benefit himself, he might be tempted *not* to exert his strongest efforts on behalf of his company!

3 *Corporate Opportunities*. The so-called 'corporate opportunity doctrine' has developed as an extension of the rules relating to secret profit. If a director takes for his own personal benefit an economic opportunity which rightly belongs to his company, he will be in breach of the fiduciary duty which he owes to his company, as he has allowed his personal interests to conflict with his duty to the company. The 'opportunity' here will include a contract for which a company is negotiating. That is so even if the company has not actually been awarded the contract at the time when the director uses his position and special knowledge to obtain the contract in question for himself (*Industrial*

Development Consultants Ltd v. *Cooley 1972*). It is irrelevant that the contract awarded to the director differs in detail from that being negotiated by the company. What is important is the similarity of the opportunity. Even if the director resigns his position immediately before he obtains the contract he may still be liable for breach of fiduciary duty and therefore liable to pay to his 'old' company any profit he makes on the contract (*Canadian Aero Service Ltd* v. *O'Malley 1973*). So, the director of a building company who submits estimates to a customer, on behalf of his company, will be in breach of his fiduciary duty if, after the customer has decided to have work done, he undertakes the job privately and keeps the payment for himself.

Only if the director could establish that the opportunity in question was one which was 'open to the world' and was not therefore a particular corporate opportunity, might he be able to take advantage of the opportunity in his personal capacity and argue that he was not 'stealing' a corporate opportunity for himself.

The director must, at all times, act in good faith in the interests of his company as a whole.

2 Duties of Care and Skill

The case of *Re City Equitable Fire Insurance Co. Ltd 1925* which established the director's common law duties of care and skill, is over sixty years old. It should be noted however that this and subsequent cases indicate that the standards probably relate only to non-executive directors and not to full-time directors who are likely to be employees of the company (see page 43). The full-time executive director will be expected to display a far higher degree of expertise – indeed, he is usually appointed *because of* his experience and knowledge!

Even a non-executive director must use reasonable care and skill in the performance of his company duties but he is not expected to be an expert in relation to the company's business. The degree of care and skill to be expected of an individual director will depend on his personal training and experience. Consequently, if the director has had little formal education and training then a lesser standard of care and skill will be expected of him than in the case of a director who is professionally qualified. In *Dorchester Finance Co. Ltd* v. *Stebbing 1977*, a moneylending company had three directors. Only one of them, Stebbing, worked full-time for the company. No Board meetings were held but the two non-executive directors were both trained accountants. The two non-executive directors signed blank company cheques which were then used by Stebbing to lend company money to his personal acquaintances. The loans were never repaid. The judge stressed the fact that the two non-executive directors were experienced in accountancy and found them to be in breach of their duties of care and skill owed to the company. Indeed the judge pointed out that they had failed to perform any duty at all as directors of the company! Stebbing, of course, was in breach of the fiduciary duty he owed to his company as well as the duty of care and skill.

If a director, whatever his background, is asked to sign a company cheque he should ask, at least, the purpose of the cheque and why the money is needed.

In an appropriate case, a director is entitled to appoint some other person to run the company business. The director is entitled to trust that person to run the company properly provided there are no grounds for suspecting that he will not do so.

Finally, the director is not bound to give continuous attendance to the affairs of the company – he is not even bound to attend all Board meetings although he should attend, if possible (and see above – *Dorchester Finance Co. Ltd* v. *Stebbing 1977*).

Remedies for Breach of Fiduciary Duty and Duty of Care and Skill

It is a well established principle that the director owes his duty to the company as a whole and not generally to individual shareholders, employees or creditors of the company (*Percival* v. *Wright 1902*). It follows, therefore, that if the director breaches that duty to his company, then the company will seek a remedy and will bring a claim, in the corporate name, against the wrongdoing director.

Exceptionally, if a director has specifically undertaken a certain task on behalf of individual shareholders, he may be said to owe a duty to the shareholders directly. It seems clear, for example, that a director may owe a duty to individual shareholders in his company, in a takeover situation. If company X makes a takeover bid for the shares in company Y, then the directors of company Y have a duty towards their own shareholders (those in company Y), which includes a duty to be honest and not to mislead. So, if the directors of company Y had been professionally advised, say by a firm of stockbrokers, that the offer price for the shares was too low and should not be accepted, the directors of company Y would be under a duty to pass all this information to their shareholders. If they did not do so, the directors of company Y, would be in breach of their duty owed directly to the shareholders. In such a case the individual shareholders concerned could claim directly against the directors, for any loss which they suffered as a result of not receiving the information about the offer price (*Gething* v. *Kilner, 1972*). The action would be brought in the name of individual shareholders, not in the company name.

Although in law there is a clear distinction between owing duties to the company and owing duties to the shareholders, in practice the distinction is often blurred.

For practical purposes, of course, the company *is* the shareholders (and see Chapter 2).

It is therefore possible for a majority of the shareholders in a general meeting of the company, to vote either to pursue a claim in the company name, against a wrongdoing director or, on learning of all the facts, to forgive a director and approve his wrongful actions by passing an ordinary resolution of the company (see chapter 4). This is known as the rule in *Foss* v. *Harbottle*, *1843*.

However, as the famous judge Lord Denning in *Wallersteiner* v. *Moir*, *1975* pointed out,

> The rule [in *Foss* v. *Harbottle*] works reasonably enough where the company is defrauded by outsiders . . . or by insiders [e.g. directors] of a minor kind. But suppose it is defrauded by insiders who control its affairs – by directors who hold a majority of the shares – who then can sue for damages? Those directors are themselves the wrongdoers. They will not authorise proceedings to be taken by the company against themselves. If a general meeting is called they will vote down any suggestion that the company should sue they themselves!

In one way or another some means must be found to prevent such an injustice. It is for this reason that there are certain exceptions to the rule in *Foss* v. *Harbottle*. The exception which is of particular importance in the case of a company which is controlled by the wrongdoing director is known as the 'fraud on the minority' exception. This enables an individual minority shareholder to bring a claim in his own name against a wrongdoing director who is the controlling shareholder, even though the company itself is unable to sue.

Where there is evidence that the director has acted intentionally or unintentionally, fraudulently or negligently *and has benefitted himself at the expense of his company*, the minority shareholder can begin a claim in his own name, on behalf of his company. This is known as a 'derivative action' – the individual shareholder derives the right to claim because of the wrong suffered by his company. In *Daniels* v. *Daniels 1978*, the majority shareholders in the company were husband and wife. They were also the directors of the company. In 1970 they caused the company to sell some land to the wife for £4,250. In 1974 the wife sold the same land to a third party for £120,000! As the company – that is the husband and wife majority shareholders – would not obviously vote that the company should sue themselves (although clearly the company suffered a considerable loss!) the minority shareholders brought a claim, in their own name, to remedy the wrong done to the company. Mr Justice Templeman held that this derivative action could be pursued in order to protect the rights of the company, as a separate legal entity. These directors were rather more than 'an amiable set of lunatics!' The judge continued, 'To put up with foolish directors is one thing; to put up with directors who are so foolish that they make a profit of £115,000 odd at the expense of the company is something entirely different!'

The small company director who is also a controlling shareholder should always remember the 'fraud on the minority' exception to the rule in *Foss* v. *Harbottle.* He ignores it at his peril!

3 Statutory Duties

The following regulations which are to be found in the Companies Act 1985 may prove to be of particular relevance to the director of the private limited company.

1 *Directors' Contracts with the Company*. As part of his

general fiduciary duty to avoid a conflict between his personal interests and his duty to the company, a director who has an interest in any contract made with his company must disclose the existence of that interest to the company in general meeting. After full disclosure, the company can vote on whether to pursue the contract or not. If the director fails to disclose his interest and the company subsequently discovers this, the company can avoid the contract in question (*Hely-Hutchinson* v. *Brayhead Ltd 1967*). In practice however, the small company director who is also the majority shareholder is making a disclosure to himself! However, because of the inconvenience of this rule – especially if the company shareholders live in several different places throughout the country – it has become common practice to include a provision in the Articles which modifies this duty of disclosure. Under Art. 85 a director *is* permitted to be a party to, or otherwise interested in, any transactions with his company provided that he discloses his interest at the Board meeting which is considering the contract (C.A. 1985, s.317). So for example, a director will be said to be 'interested' if he enters into a contract to sell some of his own property to his company or if he is a partner in a firm which is doing business with a company of which he is also a director.

In addition to the statutory penalty of a fine for any director who does not comply with section 317, the general fiduciary rules would require the director to account to his company for any secret profit which he makes on the contract.

2 *Loans to Directors*. Under section 330, Companies Act 1985, a company is prohibited from lending money to its director. This section also prohibits the company from giving any guarantee or security for any loan to

its director, even if the actual loan is made by a third party.

There are, however, several important exceptions to the basic prohibition which may be of special interest to the private company director. For example, a company can make loans to its director so long as the total amount does not exceed £2,500 (C.A. 1985, s.334).

Further, a loan can be made by a company to its director in order to provide the director with funds to meet expenditure incurred or to be incurred by him for company purposes or for the purpose of enabling him properly to perform his duties as an officer of the company. In such cases the loan should be approved by the company in general meeting or should be repaid within six months of the A.G.M. (C.A. 1985, s.337 and see Chapter 4).

Despite these exceptions, it is probable that a loan of over £2,500 by a company to its director to enable him and his family to take an exotic foreign holiday would constitute a breach of section 330! The company therefore, could avoid the transaction and the director would have to make good any loss suffered by the company.

3 *Substantial Property Transactions.* These provisions may be of more relevance to the private company which is expanding its business and increasing its capital (see Chapter 2) rather than to the newly-incorporated '£100 private limited company'.

If the company disposes of a non-cash asset to its director or acquires such an asset from its director, the transaction must be approved by the shareholders in a general meeting, if the value of that asset is more then £50,000. Even if its value is less than £50,000 but still amounts to ten per cent of the company's net assets, the consent of the general meeting is again required (C.A. 1985, s.320). So if, as is often the case, a company allows a retiring director to keep an expensive company car, the consent of the shareholders may well be required. Where such consent is required and yet not obtained, the company can reverse the transaction and claim against the director for any losses which it has suffered.

4 Directors' Share Dealings. If a director acquires or disposes of shares or debentures in his company, he must notify his company of that fact within five days. (C.A. 1985, s.328). These rules cannot be avoided by putting the shares in the name of the director's spouse or children, as this also must be disclosed.

These comprehensive disclosure provisions apply not only to outright purchases and sales but also to cases where, for example, the director has an 'interest' in his company shares – as where the director has an interest in a family trust, even though the trust itself is the legal owner of the shares.

The company must keep a register to record all the details of its directors' share dealings and this register can be inspected by members of the company and the public. If a director fails to comply with the disclosure rules, he is liable to a fine and, for continued contravention, to a daily fine!

7 Authority of Directors

If a director is properly appointed and acts within the powers given to him by his company, he can enter into contracts and transactions, on behalf of his company, with a third party or outsider. Both the company and the outsider will be bound by such contracts.

However, problems may arise if the director is not properly appointed or if the director exceeds his specific authority.

If a director's appointment is defective or if he

continues to act as a director after he has been disqualified, (see page 42) the third party can still rely on the director's actions, provided the third party has no knowledge of the defect (C.A. 1985, s.285). It should be stressed that section 285 only protects the third party in cases of a defective appointment, as where the office of the director has technically been terminated under a provision in the Articles (see page 47). It does not apply in cases of non-appointment. So if a person has been acting as the Managing Director of his company, although he has never been actually appointed as such, the third party could not rely on section 285 to enforce the contract with the company. However, that third party may be able to enforce the contract by relying on the 'Rule in Turquand's case' (see below).

If a director exceeds the authority given to him by his company – that is, he acts 'ultra vires' his own powers, even though the transaction is within – 'intra vires' – the company's objects (see Chapter 1), the company may still be liable on the contract with the outsider. Suppose the company's objects include a general power to borrow money, but the Articles of that same company impose some limit or restriction on the exercise of that power by the directors – as where the Articles require that the director must obtain the consent of the shareholders in a general meeting if the borrowing is for more than £10,000. In *Royal British Bank* v. *Turquand 1856*, it was established that, provided certain conditions are satisfied, the outsider is protected and can rely on the transaction with the company, even if the director has acted beyond the scope of his specific authority. Consequently, in the example above, even if the director negotiates a loan for more than £10,000, without getting the necessary shareholder consent, the lender should still be able to rely on the contract and enforce it against the company – if say, the company had not repaid the loan.

In order to be able to enforce the transaction with the company the outsider must have acted in good faith and be unaware of the lack of consent. There must be no question of forgery and there must be no evidence of suspicious circumstances. Further, it must be established that the director or other company officer in question, is acting within the scope of his usual or apparent authority – that is, entering into the kind of transaction, on behalf of his company, which he would normally be expected to have authority to do or which the company has 'held him out' as having authority to do. An outsider, dealing with the finance director of a company, would be justified in thinking of that director as having the necessary authority to negotiate a loan on the company's behalf – even if he had not! However, in the recent case of *British Bank of the Middle East* v. *Sun Life Assurance Co. of Canada (UK) Ltd*, the court found that a branch manager of a multinational insurance company had *not* acted within the scope of his usual authority when he represented that he could pay out large sums – up to £50,000 – on behalf of his company. Usually, such large payments would be made only by the Head Office of the insurance company. Consequently, the insurance company was not bound to honour the payments, made by the branch manager on its behalf.

The reasons for the existence of *Rule in Turquand's Case* are two-fold. Firstly, it would impose a considerable burden on people doing business with many different companies if they were obliged to check in every case whether all the internal 'machinery' of the companies had been complied with. Secondly, a company's liability is already limited (see Chapter 1) and it would be undesirable for a company to be able to limit liability even further by denying the authority of its officers to act on its behalf.

8 Board Meetings

Many private companies will have more than one director and the Articles usually provide that the powers of the directors should be exercised collectively at Board Meetings (and see page 68). The Board's powers will include the power to recommend the payment of a dividend to the shareholders, although in practice, many private companies do not declare a dividend. If the directors are also the majority shareholders they may decide to vote to themselves increased directors' fees or remuneration out of the profits of the company rather than declare a dividend on the company shares (and see page 85). Art. 70 gives directors full powers of company management for the day to day running of the business but it should be remembered that the Companies Act, 1985 requires that certain important matters must be decided by the company in general meeting – for example, where a special resolution of the company is required to change the name of the company (see page 14).

The Articles will normally contain a section headed 'Proceedings of Directors'. This section will deal with matters such as: requirements for notice of Board Meetings; the quorum required; minutes of Board Meetings and so on. Practically, the meetings of directors can be quite informal provided that the relevant provisions in the Articles are complied with.

Proper notice must be given to all the directors who are entitled to attend Board Meetings. This means simply that the notice must be 'reasonable', bearing in mind the nature and practice of business. It is obviously desirable, especially if there is important company business to be discussed, that any relevant papers should be circulated sufficiently in advance to enable all the directors to consider the proposals, attend the Board Meeting and contribute to the discussion. Art. 93 is a particularly useful provision if the directors operate in different areas of the country – it provides that a resolution in writing, signed by all the directors who are entitled to receive notice of the Board Meeting is as valid as a resolution actually passed at a Board Meeting which was properly convened and held.

The minimum numbers of directors who should be present at a Board Meeting should be fixed by the Articles but if not stated, shall be two. This is known as the quorum for the meeting (Art.89). The company Secretary should try to ensure that the proceedings before and at the Board meetings run as smoothly as possible, which will usually include the making of a record or minutes of all company meetings, including Board Meetings. This should be kept in proper minute books (Art. 100).

9 Managing Director

It is usual for the Articles to give the directors power to appoint a person to act as the Managing Director of the company. He can be appointed for such time and on such terms as the directors think fit (Art. 72). Practically any person appointed as a Managing Director should ensure that he has a service contract with his company. The contract will set out his rights and duties and he will be regarded as an employee of the company (see page 43) and *Thomas Marshall (Exporters) Ltd* v. *Guinle 1978*).

10 General Liability of Directors

In addition to the various legal duties owed by a director the company director should also note the general provision in section 310, Companies Act 1985.

This clearly states that any provision in the Articles or elsewhere, including a contract of service, which purports to exempt a director from liability for breach of duty, or negligence, or breach of trust is void – that is, of no effect whatsoever. The director may find some consolation in the fact that in any case, the English courts have power to relieve a director from liability for breach of duty or negligence if that director acted honestly and reasonably in all the circumstances. Nevertheless, the director will be considered to have acted reasonably only if he has acted in the way that a man of business with reasonable care and acumen would have acted (C.A. 1985, s.727). In recent years the courts have shown a marked reluctance to exercise this discretion in favour of the director.

Additionally, and in the light of developments in the United States, it is no longer uncommon for aggrieved company shareholders to take action and sue the director personally where they feel that he has breached the duty which he owes to his company. Because of this increasing trend and more especially because of the personal liability which can be imposed under the provisions of the new Insolvency Act (and see Chapter 6) it may be advisable for the company director to take out some professional indemnity insurance to cover himself against any such claims. It seemed somewhat surprising therefore to discover that at the end of 1986 fewer than ten per cent of the estimated 400,000 directors in the United Kingdom had insured themselves against such possible claims!

11 Company Secretary

Every limited company must appoint a company Secretary but if the private company has only one director, that same person cannot also be the Secretary

(C.A. 1985, s.283). However, if the company does have more than one director, then one of those directors can also be appointed as the company Secretary.

The functions of the company Secretary are essentially administrative rather than managerial. It is the Secretary's task to ensure that all the company documents are in order; that the company registers are maintained; that all the necessary documents are filed with the Registrar at Companies House. Additionally, the Articles usually provide that the Secretary shall conduct all correspondence with the shareholders – including sending out notices of company meetings – and that the Secretary shall be present at all company and Board Meetings to take minutes of the proceedings (see page 68).

The company must keep a record of the name and address of the company Secretary (C.A. 1985, s.290). Although the Secretary used to be regarded as 'a mere clerk' and 'a person of humble character', it is now clear that the company Secretary is regarded as an officer of the company with important administrative duties to perform. As in the case of the director, the company Secretary who does the kind of thing which he would normally be expected to do – even if he is exceeding his actual authority – will bind the company by his actions. In *Panorama Developments (Guildford) Ltd* v. *Fidelis Furnishing Fabrics Ltd 1971*, the company Secretary, B, hired cars from P Ltd, saying that they were required to carry the customers of his company. B made the hire on the company notepaper and signed the order 'B, on behalf of' his company. The hire charges were never paid because the Secretary used the cars for his own purposes. In the Court of Appeal, Lord Denning decided that the company was liable to pay the hire charges. The company Secretary is no longer a mere clerk but is an officer of the company with extensive duties and liabilities. He is to be regarded as being 'held out' by his company to have authority to enter into contracts, on behalf of his company, which are connected with the administrative side of the company's affairs – this includes hiring cars!

4 Running the Company

1 The Annual General Meeting

Each year every company must hold a general meeting of shareholders which must be specified as *the* Annual General Meeting (C.A. 1985 s.366). In the majority of small private companies the shareholders and directors are the same persons but in a situation where there are outside shareholders, the Annual General Meeting may well be the only opportunity for those shareholders to consider the performance of management, air their views and assess their investment in the company.

Proceedings at meetings of shareholders are governed by the general requirements of Company Law and the specific requirements of the Articles of Association of the company (see page 18.) The usual business of a Company's Annual General Meeting is as follows:

1 The directors must submit the accounts, (see page 69) for the most recent accounting period, to the meeting not later than ten months after the end of that period (seven in the case of a P.L.C.).
2 The accounts must contain an auditors' report which must be read to the meeting and auditors must be (re)appointed for the following period.
3 The accounts must include a Director's Report which will contain:

■ Details of persons who are, or have been, directors at any time during the period and their share-holding in the company
■ A proposal to pay (or not) a dividend

- A brief resumé of the company's trading during the period
- The principal activities of the company and any significant changes therein

4 A resolution to reappoint retiring directors (where they are required to retire by rotation by the Articles of Association) and pay their fees or renumeration.
5 A resolution to pay the auditors' fees.

It is not unknown for the directors to treat the A.G.M. somewhat flippantly and indeed, one major property company, in the early 1970s held its A.G.M. at 4.30 p.m. on New Year's Eve to cause maximum inconvenience to shareholders. The Chairman used to wear a Micky Mouse mask!

2 Resolutions

The purpose of the A.G.M. may also be to debate and vote on certain other resolutions. There are three types of resolution:

- Ordinary resolutions are passed on relatively straightforward matters by a simple majority of the members voting on the resolutions.
- Extraordinary resolutions are usually proposed to cover particularly urgent matters such as winding up the company voluntarily when it cannot continue trading because of its liabilities. An extraordinary resolution must be passed by a majority of not less than three quarters of such persons entitled to vote, in person, or, where allowed, by proxy.
- Special resolutions must also be passed by a majority of not less than three quarters (as for an extraordinary resolution) at a general meeting of

shareholders of which not less than twenty-one
days notice specifying the intention to propose the
resolution must have been duly given.

A special resolution is required in circumstances which
materially affect or alter the nature of the company, for
example, to change the company's name or to change
the objects for which the company was originally
formed (see page 15).

3 Other Company Meetings

Most business of the company, of concern to the shareholders, is conducted at the A.G.M. However, should
the directors feel it necessary, they may call a meeting
of shareholders at any time of the year giving not less
than fourteen days notice where an ordinary resolution
is to be proposed or not less than twenty one days
notice in the case of a special resolution.

4 Board Meetings

Meetings of the directors of a small private company
may well be informal affairs especially on matters
relating to the day to day running of the business but
there will be certain occasions where more formal
matters are to be decided and in that event the proceedings should be minuted. The minutes should give
details of the time and date of the meeting, the names
of directors present and the names of any other persons
in attendance and the nature of the resolutions passed,
for example, the approval of some important item of
expenditure, the adoption of accounts or the appointment of a new director.

5 Accounting Records

Every company is required to maintain accounting records which are sufficient to explain the company's transactions and to show with reasonable accuracy the financial position of the company at any time (C.A. 1985, s.221). The accounting records of the company must contain:

1 A cash book showing daily entries of all money received and spent with some narrative showing to what matters they relate.
2 A record of all the assets and liabilites of the company (Bought and Sales ledgers, nominal ledger etc.).
3 If the company's business involves the purchase and supply of goods:

- Statements of stock held by the company at the end of each financial year.
- Records of the stock count to enable the statements above to be made. One can imagine the importance of these records when one considers the importance of stock as a business asset and indeed every £1 of stock is £1 of profit.
- Records of all goods sold (other than say in a retail shop) and purchased in sufficient detail to enable the goods and the buyers and sellers to be identified. (Sales and bought day books).

Failure to keep accounting records in the above manner is an offence punishable by a fine or imprisonment or both.

6 Annual Accounts

Once a year, the directors of the company must produce to the members, at the A.G.M., an account of the

trading period in question. This consists of a Profit and
Loss Account for the year and a Balance Sheet as on
the final day of the financial year showing the assets
and liabilities of the company at that time. The annual
accounts must be filed with the Registrar of Companies
and must contain both a Directors' Report and an Auditors' Report (see below). A considerable amount of
information must be disclosed by a Public Limited
Company (PLC) but in the case of a small private
company the accounts to be filed may be modified so
that certain aspects of the company's business and
affairs may remain confidential. A small private
company for this purpose is one whose:

(a) Turnover does not exceed £1.4 million and
(b) Balance Sheet total assets do not exceed £700,000
    and
(c) Weekly average number of employees during the
    financial year does not exceed fifty. In many small
    private companies the directors and shareholders
    are the same persons and the need to report to
    oneself on the performance of the company may
    seem somewhat unnecessary. However, it should
    be remembered that these accounts are also
    necessary for arriving at taxation assessments and
    in particular so that outsiders can consider the
    company's creditworthiness.

7 The Audit

The company, at its A.G.M. must appoint an auditor
to hold office until the end of the next A.G.M. and the
auditor is required to report to the shareholders on the
balance sheet and profit and loss account produced at
the A.G.M. Before being able to report to the members

the auditor will have had to examine the company's affairs closely, scrutinising the transactions of the company, satisfying himself as to the existence of, and value of, the company's assets and liabilities. This work does, of course, incur the company in expenditure on professional fees which the small director/shareholder owned company may feel unnecessary and unjustified. The Department of Trade and Industry in its report entitled 'Burdens on Business' did in fact question the need for audits of small companies but it must be said that this is a small penalty to pay for availing oneself of the umbrella of limited liability and indeed Tax Inspectors, Bank Managers and other potential lenders derive comfort from the fact that an independent, professionally qualified person can state that the accounts give a 'true and fair view' of the state of the company and they are far more likely to rely on these accounts for that reason.

8 The Annual Return

Every year the limited company must make a return of certain details relating to itself (C.A. 1985, s.363(1)). This return must be completed within forty two days of the company's A.G.M. for that year and be signed by a director and the company secretary. The details to be included in the return are:

(a) The address of the company's Registered Office.
(b) The address of the place where the register of share-holders is kept and may be inspected (if not the same as the registered office).
(c) A summary of the company's share capital.
(d) Any mortgages and charges relating to borrowings which have to be registered with the registrar of companies. (See page 77.)

(e) A list of the names and addresses of the shareholders of the company as at fourteen days after
the A.G.M.
(f) Details of the names and addresses of the Directors
and Secretary of the company.

It is customary for the Annual Return to be filed together with the annual accounts thus making a considerable amount of information about the company's affairs
available for inspection by the general public. The fee
for filing the Annual Return is £20. Because of the
importance of this information, the Registrar of
Companies will, and does, prosecute for failing to file,
the offence being punishable by a fine.

5 Company Borrowing

Most companies are formed with the purpose of carrying on a business and, to this end, they must have money – other peoples' – to commence trading. The main sources of finance for such business ventures are as follows:

- share capital – monies or assets contributed by the members of the company in exchange for shares in the company (see Chapter 2),
- bank overdrafts – borrowing from the bank and repayable on demand,
- longer term loans – usually from banks or finance houses, repayable over a specified period, often at a fixed rate of interest with regular periodic repayments of capital,
- trade credit – obtaining goods or services on credit, or deferred payment terms whilst providing goods and services for immediate payment, in order to meet these deferred payments.

After a short period of trading the company should be generating profits from the excess of its sales over its expenditure and this becomes a most important source of finance for its future operations. Whilst not, of itself, borrowing, such a 'track record' does serve to encourage bankers and other lenders to support future business ventures.

1 Borrowing and the Doctrine of *ultra vires*

Unless there is an express prohibition in the objects clause of the Memorandum of Association, any trading company is deemed to have an implied power to borrow money incidental to the pursuit of its business. In practice nowadays most objects clauses contain an express power to borrow money.

The borrowing of money is considered to be a normal management function of directors and it is no longer usual for the Articles to specify that the directors should or must seek shareholder approval for borrowing above a certain amount (Table A, C.A. 1985).

Any person lending money to a company by way of an arrangement made with directors of the company who have apparent authority to commit the company to such a loan are entitled to rely upon that arrangement and the company cannot avoid responsibility to repay the loan because of some internal procedural irregularity (*Royal British Bank* v. *Turquand, 1886*). (See page 59.)

2 Security

Any person lending money to a company (or to anyone else for that matter!) is entitled to request a right to recourse against the property of the company in the event that the conditions of the loan are not met – that is repayment of capital or payments of interest are not met on the due dates. This right to recourse is known as security and any company with the power to borrow money has an implied power to give security for its repayment.

Where a company 'charges' part or all of its property as security for a loan and meets the terms of that loan fully and discharges its obligation under the loan then the security is said to be redeemed or discharged. Provided the company is meeting its obligation under the loan no action can be taken by the lender to realise any security he has been given. Thus, if a loan is not due to be repaid until a certain date, the security cannot be realised until that date has passed and then only if the loan has not been repaid.

Most bank lending to companies, particularly the smaller private company, is by way of overdraft – a form of lending which is repayable on demand – and this puts the banks in a strong position to realise their security immediately they sense difficulty and 'call in the loan'. The small struggling businessman will often feel that the bank should continue to support his ailing business until better times when the borrowing may well be repaid but the bank may not see matters in that light. As Mr Justice Gibson said in *Williams and Glyn's Bank Ltd* v. *Barnes, 1981*:

'I know of nothing in the ordinary contract of lending which requires the lender to share the borrower's misfortune.'

Problems as to repayment of borrowing will usually only arise when the company finds itself in financial difficulties. The remedies open to a lender in these circumstances can be detailed and will depend upon whether a charge has been given and whether or not it has been registered.

3 Debentures

A debenture is a document by which a company acknowledges its indebtedness to a lender. It will usually set out the capital sum which is repayable by a certain date and the interest payable thereon and will usually provide for the terms of payment thereof. As previously mentioned, a lender will often insist on some form of security for his loan and, if given, this will usually take the form of either a fixed charge on a specific piece of the company's property (i.e. land and buildings) or a floating charge on the whole or part of the company's assets and undertaking (business).

1 Fixed Charges

A fixed charge is a specific charge on an indentifiable asset of the company – say on land, on a ship, on an aircraft. If the lender has not been paid by the time specified in the debenture or loan agreement, he may sell the property charged and deduct what is owed to him, including all costs and accrued interest, before handing back the balance, if any, to the company. Provided that the charge is registered (see page 77) this may be done without the need to pay any preferential or other creditors (see Chapter 6).

2 Floating Charges

A company, unlike an individual, may issue a floating charge, usually over the whole of its undertaking. Because of the constantly changing nature of the undertaking (business) of a company the exact nature of the assets charged by the company are not known until the charge 'crystallises'. Thus a company may still sell assets covered by a floating charge. In the case of a manufacturing company, raw material becomes work in progress during manufacture and the finished article becomes stock. This stock is then sold to customers and the money owed becomes 'book debts', which upon payment become cash, thus generating the income to service, or pay, the loan.

A floating charge 'crystallises' when the company is unable to pay the loan and a receiver under the debenture is appointed, or the company goes into liquidation.

In some cases the charge may 'automatically crystallise' if a specific event occurs, like a breach of the term of debenture by the company. On crystallisation, a floating charge becomes a fixed equitable charge in that, at the point of crystallisation, the nature of the assets covered by the charge is clearly identifiable.

A floating charge does have some disadvantages over a fixed charge. Because of its constantly changing nature, the value of the security is not known until crystallisation and, more important still, it is repaid only after the costs of realising the charge are met and any preferential creditors paid. Lastly, unless a lender under a floating charge includes a clause prohibiting the company from creating a later fixed charge, a fixed charge, even if granted *after* the floating charge, will be paid first. A further disadvantage from a lender's point of view is that any floating charge created within twelve months prior to the start of a winding up of the company may be invalid unless it can be proved that the company was solvent at the time the charge was given or that the company received cash from the lender at, or soon after, it granted the charge in his favour (C.A. 1985, s.617 and *C T Whyte & Co. Ltd, 1983*).

In the event of more than one floating charge having been granted (i.e. to different lenders) then priority will usually rank in the order in which they are created.

4 Registration of Charges

The rules of priority of charges are, however, subject to the rules concerning the registration of both fixed and floating charges. Most charges must be registered both with the Registrar of Companies and in the company's own register of charges.

1 The company's register of charges must be kept at

the company's registered office and must show the amount of the charge, the name of the owner of the charge and a brief description of the property charged. The register must be open to the public for inspection on payment of a small fee. There is a penalty for non-registration by levy of a fine of £50 on those company officials who are knowingly parties to the breach (C.A. 1985, s.407).

2 Most fixed and floating charges created by a company must be registered with the Registrar of Companies within twenty one days of their creation (C.A. 1985, s.397). It should be noted that this is not necessarily the same date as when the loan was advanced. The Register must contain the date of the creation of the charge, the amount secured, the property charged and the name of the holder of the charge. On registration the Registrar will issue a certificate of registration which is conclusive evidence that all the requirements as to registration have been complied with (C.A. 1985, s.401 and *Re Esal Commodities Ltd, 1985*).

If a charge is not registered, or is registered late, and a later charge is registered before the earlier charge, then that later charge has priority over the earlier charge. Similarly, if a charge is not registered and the company goes into liquidation, the charge is void and the lender ranks as an ordinary unsecured creditor along with the other ordinary creditors. The importance of this is self-evident and is not lost on most lenders, particularly banks, who, in practice, will themselves take steps to ensure that their charges are registered immediately with the Registrar of Companies rather than rely on the company to do so.

5 Memorandum of Satisfaction

If a charge on any property of a company has been registered by the Registrar of Companies then, on receipt of a statutory declaration from the company, the Registrar must register any of the following facts:

- that the security has been discharged by meeting the obligation secured;
- that part of the security has been met;
- that part of the charged property has been released from the charge;
- that part of the charged property has ceased to belong to the company.

6 Retention of Title by a Seller

A contract for sale of goods may include a term stipulating that the property in the goods is not to pass to the buyer until payment has been received by the seller. These conditions are called retention of title clauses and are commonly known as 'Romalpa' clauses after a widely publicised case in England (*Aluminium Industrie Vaassen BV* v. *Romalpa Aluminium Ltd, 1976*, and see page 143).

A retention of title agreement does not constitute a charge on the property of the buying company because title to the goods does not pass to the company until the company has paid for the goods.

In order to be able to trace his property if the goods are not paid for, the seller must be able to identify his goods. This can cause problems when these goods become part of the buyer's manufacturing process and are mixed with other materials or components; say, resin which was supplied by a seller under a 'Romalpa' style agreement and mixed with other constituents in the manufacture of chipboard. The constituent parts were held to be so inseparable that there ceased to be any identifiable resin that could be the subject matter of legal title so the seller no longer had any title which was capable of retention (*Borden UK Ltd* v. *Scottish Timber Products Ltd, 1981*).

Despite such disadvantages, suppliers of goods continue to include retention of title clauses in contracts for the sale of goods.

6 Winding up the Company

The process of winding up is a formal method of terminating a company's business, paying creditors and distributing any surplus assets to the shareholders. A resolution, passed by the shareholders, for the winding up of the company will give rise to a voluntary winding up. However, if a creditor of a company presents a petition in the High Court for the winding up of the company, this will give rise to a compulsory winding up.

It will also be a compulsory winding up in any case where a petition is presented in the High Court for the winding up of the company on 'just and equitable' grounds (see page 85).

The task of winding up the company's affairs is put into the hands of a liquidator who must be a qualified insolvency practioner (I.A. 1986, s.230). It is his duty to realise all the assets of the company and if possible to pay all the company creditors having regard to any preference and any fixed or floating charges and, finally, to distribute any surplus funds to the shareholders.

Creditors who hold fixed charges over certain of the company's assets will be able to look to those specific assets, like land or buildings, to satisfy their claim. Those specific assets are realised and the holder of the fixed charge is paid off. After ensuring that his own fees are paid and that the costs and expenses of the liquidation are satisfied, the liquidator must pay any 'preferential' debts (I.A. 1986, sch. 6). These are defined as follows:

(i) debts due to the Inland Revenue for the previous twelve months;

(ii) debts due to HM Customs and Excise for the previous six months;

(iii) Social Security Contributions for the previous twelve months;

(iv) any arrears of remuneration of employees of the company for a maximum period of four months but not exceeding £800. (This amount can be changed by order of the Secretary of State.)

1 Different Types of Winding Up

1 Members' Voluntary Winding Up

If the directors and shareholders of a company no longer wish to continue the business, they may decide to wind up the company and, after the costs of the winding up, to distribute the remaining company assets to the shareholders.

However, before doing this, the directors must declare that the company is solvent and able to pay all its debts within one year of the passing of the resolution, by the company members, to wind up the company. This formal declaration of solvency must be made by a majority of the Directors and must be filed with the Registrar of Companies within fifteen days of the winding up resolution (I.A. 1986, s.89). Any director who makes such a declaration without having reasonable grounds for doing so, commits an offence. If the company's debts are not paid within one year, such a director is presumed not to have had reasonable grounds for making the declaration and he may be subject to criminal charges.

If, during the course of the winding up, it becomes obvious to the liquidator that the debts of the company will not be paid in full within one year, then he must call a meeting of the creditors and outline the true situation. At this point the members' voluntary winding up becomes, instead, a creditors' voluntary winding up.

2 Creditors' Voluntary Winding Up

This type of winding up will occur when the directors form the conclusion that the company can no longer continue to trade because of its liabilities. The directors will advise the members accordingly – very often the directors are also the company members – and will call a meeting of members who will then pass an extraordinary resolution to wind up the company, appoint a liquidator and call a meeting of the company's creditors. The creditors' meeting will then hear a report on the state of the affairs of the company and either approve the appointment of the members' liquidator or, more usually, appoint their own.

In the case of a members' voluntary becoming a creditors' voluntary winding up it should be remembered it is the liquidator who calls the meeting of creditors.

3 Compulsory Winding Up

There are several different situations in which a company may be wound up by the court but by far the most common is where a company is unable to pay its debts (I.A. 1986, s.122). One of the circumstances in which a company will be deemed unable to pay its debts is where a creditor, to whom the company owes more than £750, has served a written demand on the company, at the registered office, to pay the sum due and yet the company has neglected to pay the money within three weeks of receiving the demand (I.A. 1986, s.123).

This procedure may be of particular interest to the small business man who is having difficulty obtaining payment of his bill from his large customers. The embarrassment to the larger company of the threat of winding up proceedings being advertised might well elicit prompt payment of the bill – a useful lever for the small businessman! Further, if the small supplier attempted to obtain an actual judgement order from the court, to the effect that the money was due and payable, the larger company could defend the action and this could give rise to protracted litigation and substantial costs.

It should be noted, however, that the court will not grant a winding up order under the Insolvency Act 1986, s.123 if the debt in question is disputed by the company. In *Re Lympne Investments Ltd 1972*, Mr Justice Megarry said:

'The Companies Court must not be used as a debt-collecting agency, nor as a means of bringing improper pressure to bear on a company.'

It is for the court to decide whether there is a substantial dispute over the debt in question and, if there is, it is unlikely that the court would grant a winding up order against the company.

Another circumstance where a company will be deemed unable to pay its debts is where a creditor, having obtained a formal court judgement against a company for a debt which is owed but which has not been paid, presents a petition in the High Court for the winding up of that company (C.A. 1985, s.122). If that petition is successful, a winding up order is made and the Official Receiver is appointed as the provisional liquidator of the company.

In such a case, as the company presumably had the opportunity to defend the original action, having lost and having had judgement given against it, the fact that the judgement debt was still not paid would indicate that the company was insolvent but that the directors either failed or refused to recognise that fact and ought to have ceased trading prior to the winding up order. This may amount to fraudulent or wrongful trading (see page 86).

A limited company may also be wound up by the court on 'just and equitable' grounds (I.A. 1986, s.122). So, for example, if there is evidence that the company was being run on the lines of a 'quasi-partnership' and that 'partnership' breaks down, the court has the discretion to order a winding up of the company. The words 'quasi-partnership' recognise the fact that a limited company is more than a mere judicial entity. There is room in Company Law for recognition of the fact that behind the company there are individuals with rights, expectations and obligations. The circumstances which can give rise to the existence of a so-called 'quasi-partnership' company are:

- an association formed or continued on the basis of a personal relationship involving mutual confidence;
- an agreement or understanding that all, or some, of the members should participate in the conduct of the business;
- some restriction on the transfer of the member's interest in the company (see page 19).

In the leading case of *Ebrahimi* v. *Westbourne Galleries Ltd 1972*, E and N had been trading in partnership as carpet dealers. E and N shared equally in the management and profit of the business. In 1958 they formed a private limited company to run the business. E and N became directors and shareholders in the company. Shortly after the company was formed, N's son joined the company as a director. Together, the father and son held a majority of the company shares. The company was successful and all the profits were distributed by way of remuneration to the directors. No dividends were ever paid.

In 1969, N and his son voted at a general meeting of the company to remove E from the office of director (see page 46) and E was thus unable to participate in the running of the business. Additionally, the effect of E's removal was to deprive him of his right to share in the company profits. E was at the mercy of N and his son and if no dividend was declared on the company's shares E would receive no part of the profits of the business. The House of Lords decided that the only solution was to order a winding up of the company on 'just and equitable' grounds.

In such circumstances, particularly in the case of a small company, the winding up order would mean that the assets of the company would be divided between the shareholders so the aggrieved shareholder would, at least, get something out of the business! Naturally, if the majority shareholders and directors wanted the company to carry on trading it would be advisable for them to reach some acceptable financial arrangement with the complaining shareholder and to persuade him not to petition for a winding up of the company.

2 Fraudulent Trading

Where the directors of a company know that the company is insolvent and has no reasonable prospect of being able to pay its debts, the directors should stop trading immediately (I.A. 1986, s.213). If the company continues to trade and to incur debts when, to the knowledge of the directors, there is no reasonable prospect of those debts being paid, the court can infer that there was an intention to defraud the creditors (Re Gerald Cooper Chemicals Ltd 1978). Because of the difficulties of proving 'beyond reasonable doubt' that a director has carried on the business with intent to defraud the company's creditors, successful actions under what is now section 213 Insolvency Act 1986, have been rare. A foolish or unwise director is not necessarily a fraudulent one.

However, any person who *is* found to have knowingly been a party to the fraudulent trading may be ordered to make such contribution to the company's assets as the court thinks proper. In addition, in a serious case, the court may impose a prison sentence of up to seven years.

3 Wrongful Trading

With the introduction of the Insolvency Act 1986, the company director has never been more vulnerable to personal liability in a winding up. The concept of 'wrongful' trading has now been introduced to supplement that of 'fraudulent' trading (see above).

Basically, the court is now empowered to declare a director (or shadow director) of a company personally liable to contribute to the company's assets if he knew, or *ought to have known* that the company had no reasonable prospect of paying its due debts and that he did not take every step that he ought to have taken to minimise any further loss to the company's creditors (I.A. 1986, s.214).

In any case, where the director has doubts as to whether his company should continue trading he should seek advice from a professionally qualified insolvency practitioner. In these circumstances, independent advice should be sought, as the company's auditor will generally be precluded by his professional body from acting as liquidator. Nevertheless, the auditor should be able to recommend a reputable qualified insolvency practitioner who should give sound unbiased advice as to the next step which should be taken by the directors. He may advise liquidation or reconstruction of the company. To take and act on such advice may well be seen as a good defence to a subsequent charge of 'wrongful' trading but care should be taken to obtain advice from a reputable source.

The circumstances which lead to a winding up of a company are often, to say the least, unpleasant, particularly for the company directors if they are also the majority shareholders in the company. But, it is well known that there are some unscrupulous people who endeavour to make fortunes out of the misfortunes of others. There exists a special type of 'operator' who advertises his services especially in the Sunday newspapers, offering advice and assistance to companies in difficulties. Acting as so-called 'consultants', such people are in fact often agents for unscrupulous insolvency practitioners who advise that the company should be wound up. In the confusion, they arrange to get themselves appointed as the 'acting' liquidator of the company, until the meeting of the company's creditors.

If the creditors' meeting is delayed it is not unknown for the 'acting' liquidator to use the time to dispose of the company's assets for less than their real value. The assets are sold to nominee companies which are controlled by the 'acting' liquidator and his friends! As long ago as 1879, the Comptroller of Bankruptcy described such practices as 'organised plunder'. It is to be hoped that with the introduction of the Insolvency Act 1986, such abuses will be stemmed.

In the past, it has proved difficult to establish such frauds because embarrassed company directors are reluctant to give evidence in court. In effect they are being asked to testify as to their own foolishness and gullibility in being duped by the rogues. However, in January 1984, one such liquidation 'consultant',

Maurice Sidney Caplan – known as 'Hissing Sid' – was convicted at Manchester Crown Court for falsifying company documents. He was fined £5,000 and given a nine month suspended prison sentence.

In addition to any personal and criminal liabilities which the court might impose, it should be remembered that the court may disqualify a person for holding office as a director of a limited company (see page 42). A person may be so disqualified by the court if, following an investigation by the Department of Trade and Industry, he is deemed to be unfit to act as a director of a company (C.D.D.A. 1986, s.8).

When the provisions of the Insolvency Act came into force on 29 December 1986, one senior insolvency practitioner commented, 'In virtually every case of receivership and liquidation I have been involved in, one or more of the directors would have fallen foul of the law under the new legislation'.

The importance of these new provisions cannot be overstressed and indeed, many accountancy firms are now offering a free 'health check' for company directors who are concerned about the new legislation and the effect it could have on them and on their companies.

Part Two
The Business and Outsiders

7 The Relationship with Outsiders Generally

The principal area of law governing the relationship between a business and outsiders is the law of contract. The business will have contracts with its suppliers, contracts with its customers and, of course, contracts with its workers. The latter will be dealt with in the third part of the book. We shall see that there are other areas of law, e.g. the law of negligence, which may also be relevant – particularly where there is no contract between the business and the outsider in question. First, however, we must examine the nature of contracts and some of the rules relating to them.

The Nature of a Contract

There are many different kinds of contract, including contracts of: sale of goods, sale of land, hire-purchase, loan, carriage of goods (and people), hire, repair, building, servicing, etc. They have, however, certain features in common. First is the fact that a contract is voluntary. No-one forces X to come to a deal (a contract) with Y. Of course there may be pressures – business, economic or other pressures – but there is no compulsion. Equally there may be a lack of equality in bargaining power. So, for example, if someone wishes to travel from London to Plymouth by train, he will have no choice but to make a contract with British Rail – and on the latter's terms. Nevertheless it will be a freely entered legally binding contract.

Another feature is that a contract regulates the

position only between the parties to that contract. If British Rail break their contract with the traveller and deliver him to Bristol instead of Plymouth, it is the traveller (not his employer) who will have a possible claim for breach of contract. That is so even if the employer has suffered loss because of the traveller's delay in reaching Plymouth. Only someone who is a party to a contract can bring a legal claim for breach of the contract. Furthermore, that claim can be brought only against someone who was also a party to the contract. Suppose, for example, the delay or re-routing were caused by someone other than British Rail (say a lorry driver crashing into a railway bridge making it impassable). If the traveller or, indeed, his employer wished to sue the lorry driver (or *his* employer), it would have to be under some branch of law other than the law of contract. In this particular case the relevant branch of law would be the law of negligence and, incidentally, even that branch of law would probably be of no assistance, since it generally does not provide compensation to someone who has suffered no physical damage to himself or his property. The law of contract, on the other hand, allows a claim for purely financial or economic loss, but it allows that claim only to someone who was a party to the contract and only against someone who was also a party to it.

Someone wishing to bring a claim for breach of contract will need to show two key things: first that a valid contract was made between himself and the person he is suing (i.e. the defendant); second, that there was a term of that contract which the defendant has broken. Before looking at these matters it should be noted that a contract does not have to be in writing. With certain limited exceptions, a purely oral contract will be legally enforceable. Indeed in shops up and down the land, thousands if not millions of such contracts are made every day. Thousands more are no doubt made on the telephone. All that is needed for a contract to be enforceable is that the parties come to an agreement, that they intended it to create legally enforceable obligations and that the person suing (the plaintiff) gave something or promised to give something as his part of the deal.

The terms of a contract are the promises which the parties make to each other as part of the deal. Often there will be far more promises by one side than the other. Thus a buyer may make only one promise, namely that he will pay the agreed price upon delivery, while the seller promises all sorts of things, e.g. about specification and delivery. This does not at all matter. It is worth pointing out, though, that every claim for breach of contract is a claim for breach of promise – breach of a promise (or promises) contained in a valid contract.

Making a Contract

Offer and Acceptance

A contract is made when one side makes an offer which the other accepts without qualification. Until acceptance, neither side is bound; the side to whom the offer is made is not obliged to accept it and the offeror is at liberty to withdraw his offer. It is the moment of acceptance which signifies the making of the contract. From that moment both sides are bound. It is clear from all this that there has to be an 'offer' for there to be an acceptance of it. This can cause some difficulty. By 'offer' is meant an offer to make a contract. A contract, as we have seen, is a legally binding commitment. Thus there has to have been an offer to make a legally binding agreement or, to put it another way, a holding out, to the other side, of the opportunity (by simply accepting) of immediately creating a binding agreement. An offer is the holding out of a commitment. There is a world of difference between 'Are you interested in buying my car?' and 'Will you buy my car for £500? Say yes and it's yours.' The answer 'Yes' to the latter question will create a contract. To the former, it will not. The former question is not an offer. It is merely an 'invitation to treat', i.e. merely an invitation to negotiate and a positive answer merely allows negotiation to commence.

The test to apply in order to discover if any alleged offer really is an offer, is 'Would a reasonable hearer or reader of it understand from it that a commitment was being made, i.e. a legally binding commitment dependent only upon acceptance?' The leading authority on this matter is the famous case of *Carlill* v. *Carbolic Smoke Ball Co. Ltd* which concerned an advertisement which the Carbolic Smoke Ball Co. had placed in the *Illustrated London News*. It stated that '£100 reward will be paid to any person who contracts the increasing epidemic influenza, colds or any disease caused by taking cold after having used the Carbolic Smoke Ball according to the printed instructions supplied with each Ball. £1,000 is deposited with the Alliance Bank Regent Street showing our sincerity in the matter.' Mrs Carlill used a Carbolic Smoke Ball as directed in the instructions, caught 'flu and claimed thereby to have accepted the 'offer' in the advertisement. She therefore claimed the £100 reward. The court decided the case in her favour. Any reasonable person reading the advertisement would understand the Carbolic Smoke Ball Co. to have been making a commitment, a commitment dependent upon the reader accepting the offer by doing, as Mrs Carlill had done, what the advertisement had indicated. Of course this advertisement was unlike the majority of run-of-the-mill advertisements which would not be understood by the readers to be holding out a commitment to everyone who should choose to reply. Many advertisements are not 'offers' for the simple reason that they amount to no more than requests to their readers to respond by themselves making offers, e.g. 'Apply now to avoid disappointment', 'Instant credit available, ask our cashier for an application form', '1982 Vauxhall Cavalier, 5,000 low mileage, phone Little Muckheap 469'. In such cases a person who answers the advertisement could not claim to have accepted an 'offer' and therefore has no ground of complaint if his application is rejected or the car has already been sold. The position is similar with the display of goods (with prices shown) in a shop window. The shopkeeper is not holding out a commitment. If a customer enters the shop and asks for the goods, he is not accepting an offer. He is in fact responding to an invitation to him to go in and offer to buy. If the shopkeeper rejects the customer's offer (say by refusing to sell at the marked price) the customer has no claim for breach of a contract; no contract has been made. Although, in a case of mislabelling, the shopkeeper may have committed a criminal offence contrary to the Trade Descriptions Act 1968 (see page 152 below), that does not affect the law of contract.

Standard Forms

Some businesses have much more commercial clout than others. It may be that there is only one manufacturer of widgets, namely Widget P.L.C. In such a case, someone wishing to buy widgets may find that he has to buy from Widget P.L.C. It may be that Widget P.L.C. wishes to dictate the terms upon which it is prepared to sell. Thus it may put those terms into a standard contract document and insist that it is prepared to make contracts only upon those standard terms. The would be buyer has little choice. Either he contracts on Widget

P.L.C.'s standard terms or else he can not buy any widgets. It is a 'take it or leave it' choice.

How can Widget P.L.C. ensure that all its sales contracts *are* made upon its standard terms? One common way is for Widget P.L.C. to adopt a policy of never making an offer to sell. Thus the document which incorporates the standard terms is drafted as an offer. So when a deal is close to being clinched, Widget P.L.C. gives the form to the would be buyer and invites him to complete, sign and return the standard document. If the buyer does this, he offers to buy on the standard terms. As part of this same policy Widget P.L.C., when it gives quotations, does so in a form expressed, not as an offer but as an invitation to the person receiving it to make an offer to buy on the terms of the quotation (i.e. on the standard form). Incidentally, this is typically how hire-purchase companies and other finance companies ensure that their contracts are made only on their standard terms.

Government departments operate in a similar, though not identical, way. They, typically, invite tenders (i.e. offers) and the government will not accept any tender unless it is expressed to be an offer incorporating the standard terms designed by the government for that particular type of contract. Of course, unlike Widget P.L.C., the government will usually be a buyer rather than a seller. Problems can arise when a buyer with a lot of commercial clout comes up against a seller also with a lot of commercial clout. The government, we suppose, wants to buy widgets but only on the government's standard terms. Widget P.L.C. wishes to sell widgets to the government but only on Widget P.L.C.'s terms. Clearly if each side sticks to its policy of never making an offer, there won't be a contract. So one of them, say Widget P.L.C., gives in. It makes an offer to sell, but on its own standard terms. If the government then replies saying it rejects the offer, then again there is no contract. Suppose, however, the government replies saying that it 'accepts' the offer but does so, not on Widget P.L.C.'s terms, but on its own standard terms. According to the law of contract that reply is not an acceptance at all. Rather it is a rejection of Widget P.L.C.'s offer and at the same time a counter offer to Widget P.L.C. If Widget P.L.C. still is not prepared to accept the government's terms, it can reject the counter offer. In that case there is never going to be a contract unless either Widget P.L.C. is so keen to sell to the government that it will agree to the government's terms, or else the government is so desperate to buy widgets that the government will agree to Widget P.L.C.'s terms. Suppose, however, that Widget P.L.C. does not reject the government's counter offer. Suppose that, instead, Widget P.L.C. having received the government's counter offer, simply goes ahead and supplies and delivers the widgets. Is there a contract? If so, whose terms apply to it? The solution is that Widget P.L.C.'s actions in going ahead with supply and delivery will be regarded as an acceptance of the government's counter offer. Thus there is, in that case, a contract on the government's standard terms. It should be added that in all the above, the government has merely been selected as an example of a contracting party, albeit one with a lot of purchasing power. The law of contract applies to the government in the same way as it does to anyone else.

Bids and Tenders

The easiest way to grasp the way tenders operate is to compare them with bids in an auction room. An auctioneer, when he invites bids for any given lot, is not making an 'offer' to sell. It is obvious that the first person to 'accept' the invitation does not thereby accept an 'offer' to sell; otherwise there would be a contract made with the very first bidder. Clearly, the auctioneer is not holding out any commitment; rather he is inviting offers. Each bid is an offer and no contract of sale is made until the auctioneer accepts a bid (i.e. usually signified by him bringing down his gavel). In a similar way, someone who invites tenders does not make an offer. He simply asks for offers. Each tender is an offer. No contract is made until a tender is accepted.

The apparent simplicity of that can be disturbed. If the auctioneer has stated (in his advertisements or the auction catalogue or in what he says) that he will accept the highest bid, then he *has* held out a commitment, namely a commitment to accept the highest bid. That commitment is accepted (and thereby turned into a binding commitment) by each person who then bids. Thus if the auctioneer then refuses to knock down the item to the highest bidder, the latter will have a good legal claim against the auctioneer. Incidentally, the typical way for an auctioneer to state that he will accept the highest bid is for him to describe the lot as being 'without reserve'.

Similarly, someone who invites tenders for supplies can, in doing so, state that the lowest tender will be accepted. In that case, the person submitting the lowest tender will have a legal claim if his tender is not accepted. Normally in such a case a tender will qualify as the lowest tender only if it is a tender for a fixed sum. In other words, a tender would be ineffective if it simply stated that its price was '£10 lower than any other tender'.

There is a further problem which can arise with tenders. At first sight one assumes that if a tender is accepted, there is a contract. A tender will of course normally be written in the form required by the person who invited the tenders. Suppose then that a tender is submitted, stating a price per widget, for 'the supply of widgets during 1988 at such times, if any, and in such quantities, if any, as the buyer shall require'. This tender is then 'accepted' by the buyer. Here there is no contract since the buyer has not held out or made any commitment whatsoever. So, despite the apparent 'acceptance', there is no more than an offer, i.e. the tender. It is, however, a standing offer to supply widgets during 1988. Suppose that in January 1988, the buyer orders 100 widgets pursuant to the tender. Now, at last, the buyer is committed, i.e. to buying 100. Thus there is a contract to buy 100 widgets on the terms of the tender. The tender still remains as a standing offer. Each time the buyer places an order under the tender, a separate contract is made for the ordered quantity. Each order is an acceptance of the standing offer. The tenderer is at liberty at any time to withdraw his tender, subject only to his obligation to fulfil orders already placed under the tender before it was withdrawn.

On the other hand, a tender might indicate a price 'for the supply of 1,000 widgets, to be delivered during 1988 at such times and in such amounts as ordered by the buyer'. The 'acceptance' of such a tender would create a binding contract to sell and to buy 1,000 widgets. If at the end of 1988, the buyer had not placed orders for 1,000 widgets, he would be in breach of contract and liable accordingly.

Communication of Withdrawals and Acceptance

In some instances it can be vital to know the exact moment when a communication takes effect. For example, messages can cross each other in transmission, e.g. letters in the post. Two rules of law give rise to the problem. The first is that an offer can (at least as a general rule) be withdrawn at any time before the offer is accepted. The second is that neither party is free to withdraw after acceptance.

Let us turn first to withdrawals of offers. In order to

withdraw his offer, the offerer must notify the person to whom the offer was made. It does not matter how the withdrawal is communicated. Even if the offer was made in writing, the offer can be withdrawn by telephone. The withdrawal must, however, be communicated by one means or another and so if the withdrawal is made by post but the letter of withdrawal is (for whatever reason) not delivered, there is no withdrawal and the offer remains open for the other side to accept.

Now let us turn to acceptances. Here the rule is the same but there is an important exception. As a general rule then, an acceptance does not take effect unless and until it is actually communicated to the offerer. The exception applies only to acceptances and is known as the postal rule. Under the postal rule an *acceptance* takes effect as soon as it is posted, provided that it is properly stamped and addressed. The postal rule applies whenever it is reasonable to expect that the post will be used. Imagine that an offer is posted by X to Y just before Christmas. On January 2nd Y posts his acceptance and X posts a withdrawal of his offer. Here, since the postal rule applies only to acceptances, the contract is made on January 2nd when the acceptance is posted. The withdrawal does not take effect before it actually reaches Y and by then it is too late because the contract has already been made. The result in this example is just the same even if the letter of acceptance is delayed in the post or even if it is forever lost in the post. It is clear that, where postal rule applies, X is bound by a contract before he knows anything about it. This is not unfair to X because he could have avoided the postal rule by the simple device of stating in his original offer, that no acceptance was to take effect until it reached him. Indeed, a number of businesses have a practice of doing just that, i.e. of setting the postal rule aside. The postal rule applies to letters and telegrams and presumably also telemessages. It does not apply to other means of communication such as telex or tele-phone. An acceptance by one of these does not take effect before the message reaches the other end.

Agency

As has been seen many business are companies. When making a contract with such a business, one would not expect to deal with the company itself in person. Indeed it is a legal fiction that the company is a person. One would expect to deal with some authorised official of the company, i.e. an agent. The same will often be true even when one is contracting with a business which is not a company but which is run and owned by the owner as a sole trader or by the owners as partners. Still one would expect often to deal, not with the owner or a partner, but with an agent. Obviously, the more important the deal, the higher is likely to be the position of the agent who is responsible. One might deal with a mere sales assistant if one is buying a shirt whereas one would expect to deal with a more senior person if buying a shop. The law, however, is the same. One's contract is not with the agent but with the agent's principal. If the contract is not performed, one would therefore sue, not the agent, but his principal.

A fear which a business person sometimes has is the fear that the contract which he has just negotiated with the other side's agent might subsequently be repudi-ated by the principal on the other side. Putting it simply, the business person says 'How can I tell that this agent with whom I am dealing has his principal's authority to make this deal?'

There are three rules of law which may be of some comfort in this situation:

1 A principal is bound by any contract made by an

agent who in making it was acting within the authority *actually* given him by the principal.
2 A principal is bound by any contract made by an agent who in making it was acting within the authority *ostensibly* given him by the principal.
3 An agent who in making a contract was acting outside both his *actual* and his *ostensible* authority is himself liable for breach of a warranty of authority.

Actual Authority

It is not always easy to know the extent of the authority actually conferred upon an agent. Suppose, however, that someone is appointed to a particular position, e.g. sales assistant in Marks and Spencers, shop manager at Tesco or manager of a Watney's public house. Then, if that person is given no instructions about the extent of his authority, he will have all the authority that is *usual* for someone in the position to which he has been appointed. Clearly the sales assistant will not have authority to take on staff or to buy stock. Thus the *usual* authority of a sales assistant is normally the guide as to what is the *actual* authority of a sales assistant.

Problems can arise when the principal (i.e. in many cases, the employer) places an express restriction upon the authority of the agent. Suppose the public house manager is expressly told that he must not himself buy any cigars for the public house. In that case he clearly has no *actual* authority to make any contract to buy cigars. If he nevertheless makes such a contract, is his employer bound by it, i.e. does his employer have to pay for the cigars? The answer will depend upon whether the manager had *ostensible* authority to make the contract.

Ostensible Authority

Ostensible authority means apparent authority. In order for an agent to have ostensible authority to do something, his principal must have held him out as having that authority. His principal must have made it appear that he has that authority. If someone in the position of the cigar seller above wishes to make the public house manager's employer pay for the cigars, he must show two key things;

- a holding out (i.e. a representation) by the employer, that the manager had authority to make the contract;
- a reliance by the cigar seller upon that holding out.

As to the first of these it is not enough that the *manager* said he had authority to buy cigars. It has to be shown that his employer made that representation. This will be possible because it can be said that, by appointing him as manager of the public house, the employer has represented him to the outside world as having all the usual authority of such a manager.

The second requirement is that the cigar seller must have relied upon that representation. He can not have relied upon it, if he was unaware of it. Thus the cigar seller clearly can not rely upon ostensible (apparent) authority unless at the time of making the contract he knew that he was dealing with the *manager* of the public house. If he did know, then the manager's employer will be bound by the contract even though the manager was acting outside his *actual* authority. In this situation the agent will be answerable to his principal (here, his employer) for having exceeded his actual authority.

It is clear, then, that the common way that an agent is given *ostensible* authority is for him to be put into a position that normally confers certain authority. Consider for example someone appointed company secretary of a reasonable sized company. The fact of his appointment represents him to the outside world as having the authority that usually goes with such a position. That would certainly include authority to hire cars for company purposes. Suppose he hires a car in the company's name but for his own private purposes (say, to pick up his own mother from the airport). Can the car hire firm claim payment under the contract from the company? It would seem very unlikely that the company secretary had *actual* authority to spend company money on collecting his mother from the airport. The car hire firm is, however, able to say that they knew him to be the company secretary, that they relied upon that as giving him the apparent authority to hire cars, that the car hire firm can not be expected to investigate the purpose of any given hiring. The company is bound to pay for the hire under the doctrine of ostensible authority. The result would be different, of course, if at the time the contract was made the car hire firm knew the purpose of the hire. The company by appointing someone company secretary surely does not represent him as having authority to hire cars for non-company purposes.

Agent's Warranty of Authority

By purporting to make a contract for someone else, an agent warrants (i.e. promises) that he has that person's authority to make it. If it turns out that he did not have that authority, the agent will himself be liable. Thus in the last example, i.e. where the car hire firm knew the private purpose of the hire, the car hire firm will have a claim against the company secretary personally. By ordering the car in the company's name, the company secretary has promised that he has authority to make the contract. If that promise is broken, he is liable himself.

Other Relationships and Liabilities

Successful business involves making contracts. Much of this book is therefore given over to the law of contract. It is possible, however, to incur liabilities towards persons with whom there is no contract. One of these, product liability, will be considered in the next chapter. It is necessary here to mention some others. These are liabilities against which anyone running a business ought seriously to consider taking out insurance. In this book there is space for only an outline of some of the more common such liabilities.

Negligence

Negligence is failing to take reasonable care. There is a general and very wide rule of law that a person who is negligent is liable if, as a result, damage is suffered by someone whom it was reasonably foreseeable would suffer damage. For example, it is reasonably foreseeable that if I drive my car negligently, another road user may be injured. If that happens, I am liable to the injured person for my negligence. The position would be the same where, say, an electrician is negligent with the result that someone is electrocuted when turning on a light. The electrician is liable irrespective of whether the person injured was his own customer. The liability extends to property as well as persons. Thus if instead of a person being electrocuted, the negligence caused a fire to start and destroy the buildings and contents, the electrician would be liable to the owners for that loss.

Occupier's Liability. A rule similar to the law of negligence, applies in relation to visitors to someone's premises. Under the Occupier's Liability Act 1957, the occupier owes a common duty of care to lawful visitors to the premises. This is a duty to take reasonable care for the safety of visitors. If for example a visitor is injured because the stairs are not adequately lit, he will have a claim against the occupier under the Occupier's Liability Act 1957. Of course, the visitor could be an employee of the occupier's. For more on the duties owed to employees, see page 243 below.

Under another act, The Occupier's Liability Act 1984, the occupier even owes a duty of care towards certain trespassers. Suppose a trespasser, perhaps a child, is injured by some danger on the premises. The occupier will be liable if (a) he knew that the danger existed and also (b) he knew that a trespasser was in the vicinity of the danger. Even if he did not know of the danger or of a trespasser's presence, the occupier will still be liable if he had reasonable ground to believe these things. So, for example, if children are known to have a habit of entering the premises, the occupier must take reasonable care to prevent any of them being injured by any danger there.

Nuisance

Anyone can be liable if his activities cause an unreasonable interference with his neighbours' enjoyment of their land. For example, excessive noise, smuts, vibrations, fumes can all give rise to this liability. What is excessive (i.e. unreasonable) will depend upon various factors such as the frequency of the occurence, the duration, the time of day, the ease of reducing it and the locality where it occurs. A given level of noise might, for example, be acceptable on a trading estate when it would not in a residential area. Someone suffering a nuisance can claim damages and can also ask the court to issue an injunction (i.e. an order to stop it).

Vicarious Liability

An employer is liable for the acts of his employee committed during the course of his employment. So if a negligent driver is, say, a postman driving a post van, the Post Office, his employer, will be liable. It would be normal for the injured person to make his claim against the Post Office rather than the driver. There are two reasons for this. First it is the employer who is likely to have taken out insurance. Secondly if he has not, the employer is more likely to have the money to pay. The same would be the position if the negligent electrician above were an employee. The employer would be sued and heaven help him if the destroyed building were a city centre hotel and he does not have liability insurance cover! He is facing bankruptcy.

The rule about vicarious liability means, also, that (in the unlit stairs example) it would be no defence for the employer to say that it was all caused by some employee removing the bulbs without telling anyone.

8 Product Liability

This chapter is concerned with liability for defective or unsatisfactory goods. It is still the case that if the person complaining was himself the buyer, he is in a much stronger position than if, say, he had been given the goods. This is because the Sale of Goods Act 1979 imposes certain duties upon a trader who sells goods. Those duties are owed to the person to whom he sells. If the seller does not carry them out, then the person to whom he sold the goods will have a valid claim against him. This can result in a chain of claims. Suppose a boy buys a catapult which is defective and causes a splinter to enter the boy's eye the first time he uses it. The boy can claim against the shopkeeper under the Sale of Goods Act. The shopkeeper can in turn claim against the person from whom *he* bought, the wholesaler. The wholesaler can claim against the person from whom *he* bought, the manufacturer. Each of these claims is by a buyer against the person from whom he bought. The system can not be shortcircuited. The boy can not bring a claim under the Sale of Goods Act directly against the manufacturer. This would leave the boy without a remedy under the Sale of Goods Act if, say the shopkeeper had disappeared or was insolvent. The boy would equally be without a remedy under the Sale of Goods Act if someone else, say his mother, had bought the catapult and given it to him. Parliament has recently passed a new law making it easier for someone such as this boy to bring a claim other than under the Sale of Goods Act, e.g. against the manufacturer (see the Consumer Protection Act 1987, page 123).

In this chapter we shall look first at the seller's liability to his buyer and then at claims which can be brought against the manufacturer by any consumer (whether or not the buyer).

Seller's Liability For Misrepresentation

Anyone who makes a contract can be liable to the other party for having made a misrepresentation before the contract was made. A misrepresentation is any untrue statement of fact which was one of the causes that induced the other party to make the contract. The following, if untrue, would amount to misrepresentations: 'all leather', 'only one lady owner', 'roadworthy', 'complies with British Standard ABC 123', 'made in Britain', 'only 12,000 miles'. For the buyer to have a remedy, it is not necessary that he relied *exclusively* upon the misrepresentation. It is enough that he relied upon it to some extent in deciding to buy. Thus a buyer of a second-hand car will no doubt have a number of reasons for deciding to buy: the colour appeals to him; it drives well; there is plenty of luggage space; etc. If *one* of the reasons is that he has been told by the seller, wrongly, that it has done only 12,000 miles, the buyer has a valid claim for misrepresentation.

Misrepresentations will usually no doubt be made orally or in writing. They can also be made by conduct or by implication. Thus a car dealer who puts a second-hand car on his forecourt with the odometer showing 12,000 and with no disclaimer displayed would clearly be making a statement that the car has done only 12,000 miles.

The remedies open to a buyer who discovers that he has suffered a misrepresentation are twofold. First he can rescind the contract. This means undoing the contract, reclaiming the purchase price and handing the goods back to the seller. In order to exercise this right, all the buyer needs to do is to inform the seller that he is rescinding the contract, i.e. that he is demanding back his money. However, the buyer must act quickly. The right to rescind the contract is lost as soon as the buyer affirms the contract, i.e. does any act inconsistent with rescinding it. In practice this means that in most cases the buyer has only a few days in which to rescind. If that period elapses before he discovers that what had been told was untrue, he will have lost his right to rescind the contract, even before he was aware that he had that right!

In that case the buyer will have to look to the other remedy for misrepresentation. This is a claim for damages. The amount will normally be the difference between the value of the goods and the higher value they would have had if the misrepresentation had been true. By virtue of the Misrepresentation Act 1967, the buyer will be entitled to damages unless the seller is able to show that he (the seller) had believed, and also had had reasonable grounds to believe, that the misrepresentation was true. For example, a shoe retailer who mislabelled shoes as being 'all leather' would probably find it difficult to escape liability for damages – though in that particular example the amount would be very little.

When a claim is made against a seller for misrepresentation, it is, of course, no defence for the seller to say that it was not he but one of his sales or advertising staff who made the misrepresentation. A trader is liable for statements by his agents just as if they were his own.

A trader who (or whose employee) makes a misrepresentation might also find that he has committed a criminal offence under the Trade Descriptions Act 1968. If convicted, he could not only be fined but also be required to give compensation to any victim. That Act will be explained in chapter 12.

Seller's Liability Under The Sale Of Goods Act

The Sale of Goods Act 1979 implies certain terms about the quality of goods. These terms are therefore automatically included in the contract even though the buyer and seller have said nothing about them. The terms in question relate to description, merchantable quality, fitness for purpose and sample.

Description

By section 13 of the Sale of Goods Act, it is a condition of the contract that the goods correspond with the description by which they are sold. The description means the description which the seller has used to identify the goods. Obviously, the extent of the seller's liability here will depend upon the extent of any description he used in making the contract.

Merchantable Quality

By section 14(2) of the Sale of Goods Act, it is a condition that the goods will upon delivery be of 'merchantable quality'. The condition is automatically implied whenever goods are sold in the course of a business. The goods have to be of merchantable quality which means that they have to be as fit for the purpose or purposes for which goods of that kind are commonly bought 'as it is reasonable to expect, having regard to any description applied to them, the price and all other relevant considerations.' Much will depend upon the description by which the goods are sold. Fuel sold as 'petrol' would be of merchantable quality if suitable for use in road vehicles. Fuel sold as 'aviation fuel' would not be of merchantable quality unless suitable for aircraft. Equally, a car sold as 'new' would be expected to be of a higher standard than one sold as 'second-hand'. Similarly the price can be relevant. A mere cosmetic blemish on a new Rolls Royce might render it unmerchantable whereas it would not on a cheaper car. The standard is not an absolute one. The goods have to be *reasonably* fit for the purposes for which goods of that kind are commonly bought. With a second-hand car for example one must expect defects, though of course if the car were not roadworthy, it would not be of merchantable quality. In the case of a new car, the vehicle must be suitable for driving with the *appropriate* degree of comfort, ease of handling and pride in the vehicle's outward and interior appearance. The performance and finish to be expected are that of a model of average standard with no mileage. Any car with defective engine gearbox and oil seals would, for example, almost certainly be found by a court not to be of merchantable quality if it had been sold, with no qualifications, as being a 'new' car.

No complaint can be made, however, of defects drawn to the buyer's attention before the contract was made. Similarly, if the buyer examined the goods before the contract was made, no complaint can be made of any defect which that examination ought to have revealed.

The seller's liability for lack of merchantable quality is strict. This means that it is no defence for the seller to show that it was not his fault that the goods were defective or that someone else (e.g. the manufacturer) was the real culprit. It is no defence that the seller took all reasonable precautions to ensure that the goods were defect free. Let us return to the example where the buyer (a boy) had his eye damaged by a defective cata-pult. It would be no defence for the seller to show that the defect was latent and could not possibly have been discovered by the seller. Incidentally, in that situation the liability of the seller would undoubtedly greatly exceed the purchase price of the goods. A claim for damages can be brought at any time within six years following the breach of contract (i.e. six years from the delivery of the defective goods to the buyer).

Where goods are supplied in breach of the condition of merchantable quality, the buyer has another remedy which he may claim as well as, or instead of, damages. This right is one of rejection of the goods and will be considered a little later.

One final point about merchantable quality is that the condition relates not only to the goods but also to the packaging. That is so even if the packaging is returnable as in the case of a milk bottle. If the packaging were for example dangerous and caused injury to the buyer, he would have a claim against the seller for the goods (i.e. the packaging) not having been of merchantable quality.

Fitness For Purpose

By section 14(3) of the Sale of Goods Act, there is an implied condition that the goods will be reasonably fit for any particular purpose for which the buyer has informed the seller that he wants them. Like the condition of merchantable quality, this condition is implied only where the seller sells in the course of a business. The difference between this condition and the condition of merchantable quality is not always apparent. For example, a buyer of milk informs the seller what he wants it for, by merely asking for milk. If it happens to contain typhoid germs, it will not be of merchantable quality and equally will not be reasonably fit for the particular purpose for which it was wanted, namely human consumption. There are, however, situations where goods may be of merchantable quality and yet not suitable for a particular purpose. The buyer, for example, of a floppy disc or of a biro refill or a camera film could find himslef with a product which is in no way defective but which is unsuitable for his particular computer, ballpoint pen or camera. If at the time of purchase, the buyer had indicated the particular computer, pen or camera for which he wanted the item, the seller will be liable for breach of the condition of fitness for purpose. Again, suppose someone buys 'animal food'. Suppose the animal food supplied is suitable for feeding to many sorts of animals including all those commonly kept but that it is poisonous to mink. If the buyer had informed the seller that he wanted it to feed to mink, then the seller would be in breach of the condition as to fitness for purpose.

There is one exception to the requirement of fitness for purpose. It is that the seller will not be liable if the buyer does not rely, or it was unreasonable for him to rely, upon the seller's skill and judgement. So, suppose an exporter who is well used to dealing in Saudi Arabia buys goods in England from someone who has no knowledge of that distant land. He tells the seller that he wishes to export the goods to Saudi. When they are delivered to him and he ships them out, he learns that he can not get them into Saudi because the goods do not comply with Saudi laws. In this case the goods are clearly not suitable for their intended purpose. The seller is, however, not liable. It was not reasonable for the buyer to rely (if he did rely) upon the seller to ensure that the goods complied with Saudi laws.

The condition as to fitness for purpose is like the condition of merchantable quality in all the following respects:

- ■ Liability is strict. It is no defence that the seller was not himself to blame for the goods being unfit.

- Liability for damages can be for a much greater sum than the purchase price – e.g. if the buyer's mink all die of poisoning.
- The remedies of the buyer include the right to reject the goods and recover the purchase price.
- The requirement can relate to the packaging as much as the goods inside.

Sample

By section 15 of the Sale of Goods Act, where goods are sold by sample there is an implied condition that:

- the goods supplied will correspond with the sample,
- the buyer will have a reasonable opportunity of comparing the goods with the sample,
- that the goods will be free from any defect rendering them unmerchantable, which would not have been apparent on reasonable examination of the sample.

Buyer's Right to Reject the Goods

When goods are supplied in breach of condition (i.e. of any of the conditions relating to description, merchantable quality, fitness for purpose or sample), the buyer has another remedy which he can claim as well as, or instead of, damages. This is the right to rescind the contract and it is virtually the same as the right to rescind for a misrepresentation (see page 111 above). It is a right to reject the goods and to demand return of the purchase price. In order to exercise it, the buyer merely has to inform the seller that he is doing so, i.e. that he wants his money back. When the buyer is entitled to exercise this right and does so, he is not under any duty to transport the goods back to the seller, though of course he may choose to do so. His only obligation is to allow the seller to come and collect the goods.

As we mentioned in relation to claims for misrepresentation, this right is lost fairly soon after delivery of the goods. It is lost in each of the three following situations:

- After delivery and a reasonable opportunity to examine the goods, the buyer re-sells them.
- The buyer informs the seller that he is accepting them and not rejecting them.
- A reasonable time has elapsed without the buyer informing the seller that he rejects the goods

In the last of these, a 'reasonable time' means a reasonable time in which to try out the goods generally. It does not mean a reasonable time in which to discover the defect. The period would obviously be much shorter with a bicycle than with, say, a nuclear submarine. With most ordinary consumer goods, a few days will be sufficient in which to try out the goods generally. So if the defect does not even appear until after that, the buyer's only remedy will be to claim damages. He will have no right to demand the price back.

In practice it will only be where the defect appears very early on that the buyer will be able to exercise his right of rejection in time. If he does, he is entitled to his money back. He is not obliged to accept a credit note or substitute goods. Nor is he obliged to accept repairs. That is so, even if repairs are perfectly possible and perfectly capable of fully restoring the goods.

Liability of Non-Seller Suppliers

Some traders supply goods under contracts which are not, strictly speaking, sale of goods contracts. A sale of goods contract is one where:

- the main purpose of the contract is to transfer ownership in some goods to the buyer, and
- the price or part of it is paid or to be paid in *money*.

The following are, therefore, not sale of goods contracts: hire contracts, hire-purchase contracts, contracts to exchange goods for goods or goods for trading stamps, contracts to provide a service (e.g. a car service at a garage) where the ownership in some goods (e.g. oil and spark plugs) will be transferred as an incidental part of the deal.

The Sale of Goods Act does not apply to any of these contracts. Nevertheless there are other acts of Parliament which relate to the goods supplied under all of them. Thus in relation to the goods, the customer has rights which are virtually identical to those he would have had if he had bought the goods under a sale of goods contract. The goods must correspond to their description, be of merchantable quality etc.

Liability of Connected Lender or Finance House

Sometimes a seller will be connected with a finance company. He will have an arrangement with the finance company whereby the seller's buyer is enabled to buy goods from the seller by using finance supplied by the finance company. Indeed it may be that the seller himself introduces the customer to the finance company. Alternatively the arrangement between the seller and the finance company may be one whereby persons can use credit already agreed to by the finance company to pay the seller. This occurs in the average credit card agreement.

Where the seller and finance company have arrangements of the sort mentioned in the last paragraph, the finance company can be liable in law to the buyer for any misrepresentations or breaches of contract by the seller. This is stated in section 75 of the Consumer Credit Act 1974 and will apply where the following conditions are both fulfilled:

- The cash price of the goods in question exceeds £100 and does not exceed £30,000.
- The finance agreement between the finance company and the buyer was a consumer credit agreement regulated by the Consumer Credit Act 1974 (as to which, see Chapter 13, page 159 below).

If the buyer chooses to sue the finance company instead of the seller, the latter is not let off the hook, because the finance company has a right to recover its losses from the seller. This last right will not, of course, be of much use where the seller is insolvent or untraceable!

Manufacturer's and Distributor's Liability

Negligence

The famous case of *Donoghue v. Stevenson* was decided in 1932. In a cafe Mrs. Donoghue was bought a ginger beer by her friend. It came in an opaque bottle. Mrs. Donoghue claimed that she had drunk some and that, when she poured the rest from the bottle into her glass, out came two half decomposed snails. The case arose out of her claim that she suffered gastro enteritis and nervous shock. Since *she* had not bought the drink, she had no claim under the Sale of Goods Act. She sued the manufacturer of the ginger beer. In this case, it was decided by the highest court in the land, the House of Lords, that a manufacturer can be liable to a consumer for damage caused by negligence (i.e. the negligence of the manufacturer or any of his employees). Negligence is the failure to take reasonable care to avoid damage which it is reasonably forseeable may occur to another person if care is not taken.

In some cases it will not be easy for a consumer to show that reasonable care was not taken. If it is shown that snails were in ginger beer, a stone was in a Bath bun, a finger in some chewing tobacco, then that is strong evidence that the manufacturer or one of his employees was negligent. As it is sometimes put, 'the facts speak for themselves'. It is not always so easy. Perhaps the goods were of a type not sealed at the factory, so that the defect or alien item may have got in after the goods left the manufacturer. Then the consumer may not be able to show who was negligent. Sometimes the defect will be one which reasonable care could not have avoided. So, were the manufacturers of Thalidomide negligent in marketing that drug? An unknown undiscoverable side effect can (even if the utmost care had been taken) sometimes emerge after a drug has been marketed. There can be another, practical, problem for a consumer seeking redress from a manufacturer. The manufacturer may be abroad. Because of these and other difficulties in the law, developments are afoot. Consumers are to be given additional rights whilst the law of negligence will be left unchanged. These developments will be considered at the end of this chapter.

Two final points need to be made about negligence. First, negligence claims are not limited to personal injuries. Claims can for example be made for damage to property. Secondly, negligence claims are not limited to manufacturers and can be brought against, say, a negligent wholesaler or retailer. It could, for example, be that the retailer supplies the goods whilst negligently failing to provide the safety warnings/instructions supplied by the manufacturer. Indeed the law laid down in *Donoghue v. Stevenson* is wider even than that. *Anyone* who ought reasonably to foresee that if he is careless, someone else may be affected, owes that person a duty of care. As will be seen in the, next chapter, this can apply as much to someone providing a service as to someone supplying or manufacturing goods.

Consumer Safety Act 1978

This Act does three things. First it gives the government power to make safety regulations governing the making and supplying of goods, i.e. regulations designed to see that the goods are safe. Such regulations as have been made include those in relation to: oil room heaters, carrycot stands, electric blankets, colour coding on electrical appliances, pedal bicycles, pushchairs and fireworks. Regulations tend to be made as and when it becomes known that some particular type of goods is causing injury or seems likely to do so. It is a criminal offence for a trader to infringe the regulations. Often, however, goods reach the shops and get into people's lives before the need for regulations is perceived.

Thus the second thing the Act does is to enable the Secretary of State to take quick action by issuing one or more of three types of order:

- A *prohibition order* preventing the supply (i.e. by any trader) of a specified type of goods which the Secretary of State considers unsafe.
- A *prohibition notice* preventing the supply by a

named trader (or traders) of a specified type of goods considered unsafe.

■ A *notice to warn* requiring the trader upon whom it is served to take specified steps to warn consumers about unsafe goods already supplied by the trader

Even under the above procedure, it may take time before the Secretary of State has the necessary information to enable him to decide that goods are unsafe and that he should therefore issue one of the above orders. Thus under the Consumer Safety (Amendment) Act 1986, the enforcement authorities (i.e. trading standards officers) have power to take immediate action by serving a trader with a *suspension notice* preventing the trader from supplying goods of a particular type for a period of up to six months.

The third thing the Consumer Safety Act 1978 does is to give the consumer certain rights to sue a trader for damages. This right exists where the consumer suffers loss or damage because of an infringement by the trader of regulations under the Act or of any *prohibition order* or *prohibition notice*. This means, for example, that a child who is injured by a carrycot or pushchair because it does not comply with the safety regulations can recover damages from the manufacturer who supplied the item in contravention of the regulations. This is not really a general remedy for consumers for the simple reason that in relation to the vast majority of goods marketed in this country, there have been no safety regulations made.

Consumer Protection Act 1987

At the time of writing this book, Parliament has just passed the Consumer Protection Act which incorporates the law previously in the Consumer Safety Act 1978 and also introduces into the law a *general* duty upon traders not to supply goods that are unsafe. The Act gives a consumer who is injured by unsafe goods a right to sue the manufacturer (or importer) without having to prove negligence. Any consumer, whether the actual buyer or not, will be able to sue on a strict liability basis. The new Act, however, does not render the law of negligence irrelevant or redundant. This is because although it enables the consumer to sue for personal injuries, it does not allow claims for damage to property unless the damage is worth more than £275 and the property is mainly used for private use or consumption and is in fact intended by its owner for such private use or consumption. If the damage does not exceed £275 or if the property was for business use, the owner of it will need either to establish a case in negligence or, if he was the buyer of the goods, to sue the seller under the Sale of Goods Act.

A further, controversial, feature of the Act is that it allows a *development risks* defence, whereby the manufacturer can escape liability by showing in the case of a new product that the risk was inherent and one which could not have been discovered. It may therefore be that, even in the event of a new Thalidomide type of tragedy, the victims would have no legal remedy.

Guarantees

A guarantee will normally amount to a contractual obligation towards the particular consumer to whom it is given. Sometimes a guarantee is given by a manufacturer to a consumer who buys from a retailer. If so, it is the manufacturer who is liable if the guarantee is not complied with. If it is the seller who gives the guarantee, then the terms of the guarantee will either form part of the sale of goods contract or will be an entirely separate contract. Either way, the seller will be liable for any failure to comply with the guarantee. From the customer's point of view, guarantees have their good points and also their limitations. Their good points are that they mean that defective goods are usually put right without any quibbling. Their limitations are that usually they give no right to recover the purchase price and usually they do not cover consequential loss or damage. Thus the buyer who wants his money back will need either to persuade the seller to refund it as a matter of goodwill or else to be able to rely upon the limited right to reject the goods for breach of one of the conditions in the Sale of Goods Act. The consumer who wishes to recover damages for consequential loss (whether personal injuries or damage to property) will need to rely on the law covered earlier in this chapter.

Where a consumer is given a guarantee, that guarantee (whatever it says) can not remove or reduce the consumer's rights (a) to have his remedies under the Sale of Goods Act or (b) to claim for any personal injuries caused by negligence. Here we are talking about exclusion clauses. These will be covered in chapter 10.

Loss of Profits

So far in this chapter, we have envisaged the liability of a business to an ultimate ordinary private consumer who has found the goods dangerous or defective. Goods are, however, often sold by one business to another not for onward sale but for use in the latter business. Then the seller can be liable to the buyer in much the same ways as mentioned earlier, e.g. for any misrepresentation, for the goods not matching their description, not being of merchantable quality etc. In addition, in a contract between businesses, there is much more likely to be a written contract including further terms. If any one of these is broken, the party breaking it will be liable to the other. In a claim for breach of contract (including claims for breach of the conditions in the Sale of Goods Act), a claim for damages can include a claim for loss of profits. The buyer therefore does not have to show any personal injury or damage to property. Suppose a mink farmer bought 'mink food' which was not at all toxic to mink but merely stopped the mink from breeding for a while. If the farmer could show that this was because the food had not been of merchantable quality, he could claim for his loss of profits, i.e. loss of production of mink.

Generally speaking, a claim purely for loss of profits can not be made either in negligence or under the Consumer Protection Act.

9 Services

A wide variety of services is provided by a wide variety of businesses. The obligations of the various suppliers will vary enormously. The reason is simply that the contracts they make will themselves vary enormously. All that can be said is that the supplier can be liable under any one of three main headings: for breach of an express term of the contract, for negligence or for misrepresentation.

Express Terms of the Contract

If the supplier breaks an express term in the contract he is liable to pay damages for any loss thereby occasioned to his customer. If it is a breach so serious that it deprives the customer of substantially the whole benefit of the contract, the customer will even be entitled to refuse to go on with the contract.

Implied Terms of the Contract and Negligence

The Supply of Goods and Services Act 1982 implies certain terms into contracts. Firstly any *goods* supplied under the contract (e.g. spare parts provided under a contract of repair) are subject to implied terms which are the same as those which apply when goods are sold for cash. Those terms, as to description, merchantable quality etc, were explained in Chapter 8. Secondly, as regards the services provided, there is an implied term that the supplier of the service will carry it out with reasonable care and skill, i.e. that he will not be negligent. This means that someone who is dissatisfied with the standard or quality of *service* he has received has to show either that there is some express term of the contract which has not been complied with or else that the supplier has been negligent. Claims for negligence can therefore be made against virtually anyone providing a service: laundries, watch repairers, carpet layers, architects, solicitors, doctors, plumbers, electricians etc. This list is endless.

Normally the person making the claim will be the customer, i.e. the person who made the contract with the supplier of the service and who agreed to pay for it. However, if someone else suffers injury or damage because of the negligence, he could also have a claim. Suppose a householder has his roof re-tiled and that that tiler is negligent in doing the work with the result that a tile subsequently falls upon a person who is visiting the house. This victim could claim against the tiler (or the tiler's employer) because of the tiler's negligence. Indeed, turning to doctors, most claims for negligence against doctors will be made by people who have no contract with the doctor. That is for the simple reason that instead of making a contract with the doctor, most people are treated under the N.H.S.

If one's only loss is monetary and there is no physical damage to person or property, the position is not so straightforward. Of course, that is unlikely in the case of a patient. Suppose, however, that service engineers are engaged to service the filters of a fish breeding aquarium and that they do the work negligently. If the fish die as a result, that is physical damage and the owner of the fish has a right to make a claim irrespective of whether it was he who made the contract with the service engineers. If, however, the negligence did not damage any fish but simply caused the aquarium to be closed and the fish owner to have to resort to another, more expensive aquarium, the story would be different.

It would matter who had made the contract with the service engineers. If it was the fish owner, he would be entitled under his contract to recover from them his financial loss. If it was someone else (say the aquarium owner), it is unlikely that the fish owner would be entitled to recover his loss, as it was entirely financial and not physical.

Time of Completion

If a contract does not stipulate a date for performance or completion of the work, then it must be completed within a reasonable time. This makes it often very difficult to know whether the supplier of the service is in breach of contract or not.

Payment of the Price

In the case of a lump sum contract (i.e. where a definite fixed sum is agreed), if there is no agreement as to when it is payable, it is not due until the work is completed. Unless expressly agreed otherwise, there is no right to any advance payment. Also if the supplier of the service abandons the work half way through, he is not entitled to any of the agreed price.

Sometimes no fixed price is agreed. This commonly occurs when someone has his car serviced at a garage. In that case a reasonable sum is payable for such authorised work as is done. Thus if the garage carries out some of the authorised repair work but not other of it, the garage will be entitled to a reasonable sum for the work actually done. A reasonable sum is likely to be judged by reference to what is the going rate in the trade.

Incidentally, certain traders have a *lien* over goods. That is a right to retain possession of the goods until payment has been made. For example a hotel or inkeeper can impound and retain luggage of a guest who fails to pay. Similarly repairers and improvers have a lien on the goods they have repaired or improved. They are entitled to retain them until paid what is due to them.

Misrepresentations and Trade Descriptions

A trader providing a service can be liable for misrepresentation in just the same way as a trader selling goods (see page 111). It is also possible for a trader providing a service to commit an offence by making a false trade description. Those traders most commonly caught include travel and holiday firms. Trade descriptions law will be considered in Chapter 12.

Connected Lender Liability

A supplier of services may have an arrangement with a finance company whereby the supplier's customers are enabled to pay the supplier for his services by using finance provided by the finance company. We have seen (page 119) that a seller of goods often has such an arrangement and that the use of credit cards involves just such an arrangement. The only difference is that here we are talking about services (e.g. car servicing, clothes laundering, watch repairs, garden landscaping). The legal position is the same here as it was with goods. It is that the finance company can be liable to the customer for misrepresentations and breaches of contract by the supplier. This will be the case where two conditions are both present:

1 The cash price of the services in question exceeds £100 and does not exceed £30,000.
2 The credit agreement between the finance company and the customer is one which is regulated by the

Consumer Credit Act 1974 (see pages 119 above and 173 below).

10 Exclusion Clauses

An exclusion clause is a term put into a contract to exclude or restrict the liability of one of the parties. Until recent years it was possible for such a clause to exclude virtually all the terms implied into the contract for the benefit of the customer and to exclude liability for negligence and misrepresentations as well. This would often leave the customer without a remedy for defective goods or poor or negligent services. There were only two requirements for the clause to be effective. Firstly, it had to be part of the contract. Secondly, it had to be clear. These requirements were, however, easily satisfied.

Part of The Contract

In the case of a written signed contract, it was easy to make the clause part of the contract. It only had to be legibly printed as part of it. The customer did not need to have read it. It would still be part of the contract.

Where a contract was not written, say in the case of a purchase of a new pair of shoes or a stay in a hotel, an exclusion clause could still be part of the contract. It simply had to be displayed prominently at the spot where the contract was made, i.e. at the point of sale or, in the case of the hotel, at the reception or signing in desk.

Clarity of the Clause

Certain businesses and their lawyers became adept at writing exclusion clauses. So in a sale of goods contract a buyer might find he had signed a contract containing some clause like:

> *All express or implied conditions and warranties, statutory or otherwise are hereby excluded. The seller does not accept any liability for misrepresentations or negligence or for any consequential loss howsoever caused.*

Such a clause would almost certainly have left the buyer with no effective remedy against the seller if the goods proved defective.

The Unfair Contract Terms Act 1977

Parliament came to recognise that because of the increasing use of exclusion clauses (or disclaimers as they were sometimes called) large numbers of customers of all sorts of businesses were being left without a remedy when they received defective goods or services. The Unfair Contract Terms Act 1977 was passed to control exclusion clauses. Even after the Act, it is still the law that a clause will be ineffective unless it is part of the contract and its wording is clear. Today, however, even if the clause is both part of the contract and also clearly worded, it will not work if the 1977 Act makes it ineffective. This Act works in two ways. Firstly, it makes some exclusion clauses automatically totally ineffective. Secondly, it makes a lot of other exclusion clauses ineffective unless they pass a test of reasonableness.

Totally Ineffective Exclusion Clauses

There are three types of clause which will not work in any circumstance. They are automatically ineffective.

1 A clause trying to exclude or limit anyone's liability for personal injuries or death caused by negligence.
2 A clause trying to exclude or limit liability, under a sale of goods contract or similar contract, for breach of the implied term as to title.
3 A clause, in a contract with a consumer, trying to exclude or limit a business's liability for breach of the implied terms as to: description, merchantable quality, fitness for purpose and sample.

The first of these means that, for example, a clause saying 'Passengers travel at their own risk' can not prevent a passenger from being entitled to recover damages from a person who negligently causes him personal injuries. The second deals with the obligation of a seller in relation to the ownership of goods. The buyer expects to become the owner. If it should turn out that after all the seller did not own the goods, the buyer may find that he has to surrender the goods to their true owner. In such a case the seller is liable to the buyer for breach of an implied condition as to title. This liability can not be excluded or limited.

The third category above deals with the implied conditions, in sale of goods (and certain other) contracts, relating to description, quality and sample. These conditions were explained in Chapter 8. Liability for breach of them can not be excluded or limited in any contract where the buyer is an ordinary consumer. This means where the buyer is buying goods which are ordinarily bought for private use or consumption and is not buying them for business purposes (or at an auction or by competitive tender).

Where there is a contract with an ordinary consumer,

not only would the clause be ineffective if it tried to exclude the seller's liability for breach of one of the implied conditions. Also the seller would be guilty of a criminal offence if he included the clause in the contract, displayed it in his shop or attached it to the goods. Suppose an ordinary retail shop contained the sign 'Sale goods are in no circumstances returnable'. The shopkeeper would commit the criminal offence just mentioned. Even 'sale' goods can be of less than merchantable quality or not matching the description given them. If so, a buyer would be entitled to reject the goods and recover the price. A clause claiming to take away that right will not work and the trader responsible for it will be guilty of the criminal offence mentioned.

Clauses Subject To The Reasonableness Test

An exclusion clause is subject to the reasonableness test if it is one of the standard terms used by the person it is trying to protect. An exclusion clause will also be subject to the reasonableness test if it tries to exclude or limit any of the following:

1 Liability for misrepresentation
2 Liability for loss or damage (other than death or personal injury) caused by negligence
3 Liability to a non-consumer for breach of the implied terms as to description, merchantable quality, fitness for purpose and sample.

Clauses which have already been described as totally ineffective will not, of course, be subject to any test of reasonableness. They are ineffective and that is the end of the matter.

It will be clear that virtually every other exclusion clause will be subject to the reasonableness test, since virtually every exclusion clause *is* part of the standard terms of the party it is trying to protect. 'Standard terms' simply means the terms that someone habitually or regularly uses in his contracts.

Number 2 in the list above makes it clear that there is a difference between personal injuries and other damage or loss caused by negligence. Liability for the former can never be excluded or restricted. Liability for the latter, say for loss of luggage, can be excluded by a clause which satisfies (passes) the reasonableness test.

Number 3 in the list makes clear another difference, namely the difference between a buyer of goods who is an ordinary private consumer and one who is buying for his business. Liability to the former for breach of the conditions as to description, merchantable quality etc can never be excluded. Liability to the latter for such breaches can be excluded or limited by a clause which satisfies the reasonableness test.

The Reasonableness Test

In the case of a dispute, it will be the court, i.e. the judge or arbitrator, who will decide whether or not a clause passes the reasonableness test. A clause which fails the test is ineffective. The court will take into account the following sorts of factors:

1 *Whether the customer could easily have covered the risk in some other way.* So for example a furniture removals firm might have in its contract a clause excluding liability for any loss or damage to the furniture. If the firm at the same time offers the customer the chance of taking out insurance, at a reasonable price, against the risk of loss or damage, that might well mean that the clause passes the reasonableness test.

2 *Whether the same goods or services were available without such an exclusion clause.* If, for example, other furniture removals firms would have charged much the same

and did not have such an exclusion clause, then the customer would have had a real choice whether or not to accept the clause. That would tend to help the clause to pass the reasonableness test.

To take a different example, a farmer may buy seed potatoes on standard terms which limit the seller's liability to a maximum figure which equals the purchase price. If in fact he could have bought them elsewhere at the same price and without such a limitation of liability, the limitation clause will pass the reasonableness test. If subsequently the seed potatoes fail to produce a crop, the farmer's loss will, no doubt, vastly exceed the cost of the seed potatoes. However, having contracted subject to the limitation of liability, he will be able to recover no more than the purchase price which he paid.

3 *Whether the clause tries totally to exclude liability or merely limits it to a fairly high maximum figure*. A clause which merely places a maximum figure on liability is much more likely to pass the reasonableness test.

4 *Whether the clause lays down some unreasonable condition*. A clause might, for example, exclude 'all liability for defects and defaults other than those notified within two days of delivery'. This would not pass the reasonableness test.

It should finally be observed that the burden of proof lies upon the party who wishes to rely upon the clause. This means that the clause will be assumed to be unreasonable (and therefore ineffective) unless that party can show it to have been a reasonable clause to have included in the contract.

Guarantees of Goods

The effect of guarantees has already been discussed in chapter 8 (see page 124). In short, a guarantee will confer rights (according to its terms) upon the buyer which are additional to those he would otherwise have. In days gone by, however, it used to be common for a guarantee not only to confer certain rights (e.g. of repair or replacement) upon the buyer but also at the same time to exclude or limit his rights under the implied terms of the Sale of Goods Act (i.e. as to description and merchantable quality etc.). It would take away more, much more, than it gave. As we have seen, such a provision can not now possibly have any effect where the buyer is an ordinary private consumer. We have also seen that it is a criminal offence to include any such thing in the guarantee. The law goes further even than that. It is a criminal offence to supply goods with any guarantee or statement about liability for description, quality or defects, unless that guarantee or statement also makes it clear that it does not affect the statutory rights of the consumer.

11 Ownership, Risk, Delivery and Payment

It may be obvious that someone involved in buying or selling goods will have an interest in sorting out what his rights and duties are as regards delivery and payment. He should also have a very great interest in sorting out exactly when *ownership* in the goods and the *risk* of accidental loss or damage to them are to transfer from the seller to the buyer. There is no automatic rule that these two things transfer at the same time as the goods are delivered. We shall look first at the transfer of ownership (i.e. title).

Ownership

If goods are being bought, it is obvious that the whole object of the transaction is that the buyer is to become the owner of them. But when? The answer to this question could in some circumstances be vital for the buyer or seller. First, there is a general rule that, unless otherwise agreed by the parties, goods are (so far as accidental loss or damage is concerned) at the risk of the owner. To put it another way, unless the parties agree otherwise, risk transfers to the buyer when ownership transfers. Thus if the goods are lost or damaged, the issue as to whether it is the buyer or the seller who has to beahe loss will depend upon whether ownership had at the time already transferred to the buyer. We shall return to risk again a little later.

The second circumstance in which it might be vital

to know whether ownership had transferred is in the
event of the bankruptcy of either the seller or buyer.

Bankruptcy of Buyer. If, before being paid, the seller has
not only delivered the goods to the buyer but has also
transferred ownership to the buyer, the seller is in an
exposed position in the event that the buyer goes bankrupt before paying. In that case, the seller has a valid
claim for the price but is a mere unsecured creditor of
the buyer. If, on the other hand, the ownership had
not transferred to the buyer before he went bankrupt,
the seller could take the goods (i.e. *his* goods) in priority
to the buyer's other creditors.

It follows from all this that, where the seller gives
the buyer credit, it is a good idea for the seller, if he
can, to organise the contract terms such that he remains
owner until payment is complete. We shall return to
retention of ownership (title) clauses a little later.

Bankruptcy of Seller. If the buyer makes payment or part
payment before taking delivery, he may be in an
exposed position in the event that the seller goes bankrupt before delivery. In that case the buyer will have a
valid claim against the seller for non-delivery but will
be a mere unsecured creditor unless the ownership had
already transferred to the buyer. If it had, the buyer
will be entitled to take the goods (i.e. *his* goods) in
priority to the seller's other creditors.

Unascertained Goods

There is a crucial difference between specific goods and
unascertained goods. Specific goods are goods which
at the time of the contract are identified and agreed
upon. It may be possible, at the time of the contract (as
in the case, say, of a sale of a second-hand car) to point
to the goods and say 'Those are the goods which are

being sold under the contract'. If so, the goods are specific. Suppose, on the other hand, that an order is placed (i.e. a contract is made) for the sale of some goods by description (e.g. 'a bottle of Taylor's 1976 vintage Port' or '100 yards of Liberty's curtain material Roses Pattern number 1461' or 'a new Royal Blue Ford Sierra 4 door saloon GT model' or '10 gallons of 4 star petrol'). In these cases the buyer can certainly say he has 'ordered' the goods but, at the time the contract is made, it is impossible for him to point to any particular goods and say of them that they are the goods he is buying. The goods are unascertained. It is impossible for ownership in unascertained goods to transfer to the buyer at the moment the contract is made. The ownership can not transfer because it is impossible to know to which particular goods reference is being made.

The normal rule is that ownership in unascertained goods will transfer to the buyer when one party (usually the seller) with the consent of the other (usually the buyer) appropriates goods of the correct description to the contract. In the case of petrol this may occur only a few moments after the contract is made. The buyer asks for ten gallons of 4–star. The seller – or, rather, his salesman – agrees (thereby accepting the buyer's offer and making a contract). The seller then a moment or so later puts the ten gallons into the buyer's petrol tank thereby appropriating that particular ten gallons to the contract. In the case of the new Ford Sierra, the delay may be much longer. The seller may have to order one from the manufacturer.

In the case of unascertained goods there is not a lot the buyer can do to safeguard himself against the risk of the seller's becoming bankrupt. The obvious thing, of course, is not to agree to pay over any money until the seller delivers the goods to the buyer. The seller may, however, simply refuse to make the deal on such terms. This sometimes occurs where the seller will have himself to spend money on the contract long before delivery to the buyer is to take place. This will be the position where the seller is to make the goods, say a ship, to the buyer's order. At the time of the contract the seller wants a down payment and he wants further stage payments as the work progresses. At the time of the contract the work has not even begun. So a term of the contract saying that ownership in the ship transfers immediately to the buyer will not work, for the simple reason that there is no ship. In this situation, probably the best that the buyer can achieve is a clause saying that, from the moment construction begins and at all stages throughout construction and thereafter, the vessel (and all materials used, or appropriated for use, in its construction) shall be in the ownership of the buyer.

Specific Goods

We have seen that these are goods which are identified and agreed upon at the time the contract is made. This is the situation with virtually every sale of a second-hand car. It is also the case where goods are sold at auction. There is a general rule applying to specific goods to which nothing remains to be done to make them fit and ready to deliver under the contract. It is that, unless otherwise agreed, the ownership transfers to the buyer at the moment the contract is made. In the case of a sale by auction, that is when the gavel comes down. It may be, on the other hand, that the seller has in the contract agreed to do something to the goods before delivery. The second-hand car seller may, for example, have agreed to respray the bonnet or to replace the clutch. If so, ownership will not transfer to the buyer until the seller has carried out the work and then given the buyer notice of that fact. There is a similar rule where the seller has agreed to weigh, test or measure the goods for the purpose of ascertaining the price.

For goods delivered on approval or on sale or return terms, the rule is that ownership does not transfer to the buyer until either the buyer signifies his acceptance (or approval) or he keeps the goods beyond the stipulated time for their return. If there was no fixed time stipulated, then the period of time allowed is a reasonable one.

All of the above rules can be altered by agreement of the parties at the time the contract is made.

Retention of Title Clauses

A seller who lets his buyer have goods on credit terms may well consider having in the contract a clause stipulating that the goods are to continue to belong to the seller until they are paid for. By retaining title (i.e. ownership) until he is paid, the seller safeguards himself against the buyer becoming bankrupt before paying. If the buyer becomes bankrupt, the seller is entitled to take the goods in lieu of payment. The problem is exactly the same where the buyer is a company, for a company can go into liquidation or have a receiver appointed, just as an individual can go bankrupt.

A seller will tend to think about this problem when he is regularly supplying goods to the same buyer. In that case the seller can find himself at any one time in a position where several consignments have been delivered to the buyer but not yet paid for. From the seller's point of view, there are two drawbacks from the apparent simplicity of a retention of title clause. First, the buyer may well wish to sell the goods. Indeed it may be that it is only by selling the goods that the buyer is able to maintain payments to the seller. So it

is in the seller's interest not to limit the buyer's ability
to re-sell. That means that the seller will, at the moment
of resale by the buyer, have to surrender his ownership.
This is because no-one will want to buy from the buyer
if he is not himself to become the owner of the goods.
The retention of title clause therefore says that the
goods remain in the ownership of the seller until *either*
the seller has been paid for them *or* the buyer re-sells
them. Thus the buyer has constant turnover in his stock
which (so long as he has not paid the seller for it)
remains in the ownership of the seller until the buyer
sells it. This means that it is quite possible for the buyer
to be in possession of a lot of stock-in-trade, the vast
majority of which he does not own.

By way of an aside, one can observe that this could
make it difficult for the buyer to raise finance. If the
buyer is a company, one way of raising a loan, say from
a bank, is to give the lender a floating charge over
the company's assets (see page 76 above). If the vast
majority of its apparent assets are not in fact owned by
the company, the value to the bank of having a floating
charge would be virtually nil.

Look at matters again from the seller's viewpoint.
The seller loses ownership when the buyer re-sells the
goods and the buyer therefore has a regular turnover
in goods which (so long as the buyer has them and has
not resold them) belong to the seller. For this reason it
is common for a retention of title clause to state that
goods supplied to the buyer remain (until resold by the
buyer) in the ownership of the seller so long as *any*
money in respect of *any* consignments remains owing
to the seller.

There is another complication which can disturb the
apparent simplicity of a retention of title clause. It arises
in circumstances where the buyer, instead of simply re-
selling the goods, uses them up or converts them in
some industrial process. Examples might be fuel oil

used in heating or yarn turned into material, leather turned into handbags, wood turned into furniture. In these cases the goods are either destroyed (e.g. fuel oil being burned) or have their character completely changed and submerged in something else. If they are destroyed then nobody can own, or retain the ownership in, them. In the event of the buyer's bankruptcy or liquidation, the seller would be able to take only the unconsumed goods in priority to the other creditors. If the goods have their character completely changed and submerged or converted into something else, then new goods (e.g. handbags) have been created and the old goods (e.g. the leather) no longer exist. Since the old goods no longer exist, no-one can have retained any ownership in them. Again, in the event of the buyer's bankruptcy or liquidation, the seller could take in priority to the other creditors only such of the old goods (e.g. the leather) as were unused.

Suppose that the seller has foreseen this problem and has written, in the retention of title clause, that, upon the goods being converted in a manufacturing or industrial process, the seller's ownership is to transfer to the newly produced goods (e.g. the handbag). This could not be described as *retaining* title in goods but as *acquiring* title in new goods. That provision amounts to a *charge* over assets of the buyer and will be void (i.e. valueless) unless registered by the buyer (see page 77 above).

Risk

We are talking here about the risk of the goods being lost, stolen, destroyed or damaged. Whose loss is it, the seller's or the buyer's?

General Rule

The general rule, under the Sale of Goods Act, is that the risk passes with the ownership. There are two qualifications to that. First, if the damage or loss is attributable to the negligence of the buyer or seller, then the negligent party bears the loss. Second, if the goods were late being delivered because of the fault of either party *and* the loss or damage might not have occurred but for the delay, the loss falls on the party at fault.

Agreement Otherwise

The general rule can be altered by the parties agreeing otherwise in their contract. It would often be sensible to make specific provision in the contract for the transfer of risk. Suppose the goods are to be delivered (a) by the seller or (b) by an independent carrier such as the Post Office or National Freight Carriers. Who is to bear the risk of loss or damage en route? If the parties do not specify then the answer will depend upon when ownership passes. That in turn may well depend upon whether the goods were specific or unascertained (see above). It is better to specify in the contract who is to bear the risk. It may then be that the party at risk will wish to insure the goods. It should be pointed out that in a situation where a seller agrees to deliver the goods 'at his own risk', the buyer will still have to bear the risk which is normally incidental to the course of transit. Thus if it is intended that the seller should shoulder *all* risks, including those normally incidental to the course of transit, the parties will need to spell that out very specifically in the contract.

Now consider again the shipbuilding example, given earlier, where the parties agree that ownership in the vessel as and when it is built will be the buyer's. Nevertheless, the vessel will be in the seller's shipyard. It would be daft not to state in the contract that the risk does not pass with ownership, but remains with the seller until delivery. After all, he is in a position to take care of the vessel and likely to be insured (or to get insurance cover) against the risks.

Again, consider a retention of title clause. The buyer is in possession of goods belonging to the seller. The seller would be silly not to provide in the contract that risk passes to the buyer upon delivery to the buyer (i.e. before ownership passes). It is clearly sensible that the buyer and not the seller should expect to insure the goods.

Delivery and Payment

Delivery

It is the seller's duty to deliver the goods to the buyer. 'Deliver' does not mean, however, transport. It simply means 'hand over'. In other words, unless the parties have agreed otherwise, it is not for the seller to arrange transport to the buyer. It is for the buyer to collect the goods.

Payment

If the parties do not state otherwise in the contract, there are two basic rules. The first is that payment is due when ownership in the goods passes to the buyer. The second is that payment and delivery are concurrent conditions of the contract. This means that when the buyer turns up to collect, the seller is entitled, unless the contract says otherwise, to say 'I am not handing over the goods unless you pay me for them at the moment of the hand over'. Of course a lot of sellers would not insist upon their rights in this way and would be quite happy to allow the goods to be collected and to invoice the buyer later. In doing that, the seller is in fact allowing the buyer to have credit when that was not part of the contract. Unless he has agreed to that in the contract, the seller does not have to allow it. He has a right to exercise a *lien* over the goods, i.e. to refuse to part with possession except against payment. He has that right, even if (on the rules examined earlier) the ownership in the goods has already passed to the buyer.

12   Advertising

There are various pieces of law which an advertiser might find himself breaking. He might, in putting a leaflet under the windscreen wiper of someone's car, scratch the windscreen thereby exposing himself to a civil claim for damages by the car owner. He might place a poster on someone's wall without permission, again exposing himself to risk of a civil suit. He might find himself infringing specialist legal rules relating to advertisements of particular types of things, e.g. betting and gaming, investments, food, drugs and medicines. There is no room here to deal with all these different things – though credit advertisements are referred to in the next chapter. In this chapter we shall examine only those general bits of law which almost any advertiser ought to have in mind when considering (a) his sales promotions methods and (b) the content of his advertisements and labelling. It is not intended to deal with passing-off (i.e. making it appear that your goods or services are in fact those of another business), or infringing trade marks and copyrights.

Unsolicited Goods, Free Samples etc.

The Unsolicted Goods and Services Act 1975 banned a particular method of inertia selling, namely the practice of sending goods to someone who had not asked for them and then following that with a demand or request for payment for them. Under the Act unsolicited goods are treated in law as an unconditional gift to the recipient if they have not been re-collected from him within six months of him receiving them. If he does not want to give them house room for that long, he can serve a notice on the sender and they will then become an unconditional gift after a month from that notice. Of course, someone demanding payment for unsolicited goods is demanding payment to which he must know he is not entitled. The Act makes that a criminal offence.

The Act does not ban the sending of free samples. These are clearly intended as gifts anyway. Nor does it ban distributing free literature. In this connection there are, however, two controls to watch out for. First, the 1973 Act makes it a criminal offence to send unsolicited advertising material for any book, magazine or leaflet which describes 'human sexual techniques'. Second it is a criminal offence to send to anyone under eighteen a leaflet or circular advertising the availability of credit or goods on hire (see page 168 below).

Doorstep Canvassing

There is no general ban or control on this practice, except where credit or goods on hire are being offered. The controls on these are explained in the next chapter. The whole issue of doorstep selling is, however, a sensitive subject. Selling to someone by visiting them in their home can involve high pressure selling and that can give a bad name to the whole exercise. In the case of contracts made by a customer away from the trade premises of the seller (i.e. usually in the customer's own home), there is no general right to a 'cooling off' or cancellation period. That right exists only where the agreement is a credit or hire agreement regulated by the Consumer Credit Act. Nevertheless there are some firms which, as part of the contract, expressly give the customer such a right even in the case of cash deals.

This is commonly done by building and double glazing firms who are members of trade associations whose codes of practice require them to do so. A lot of mail order firms do likewise, giving the customer the right to return the goods within a few days thereby cancelling the deal.

The European Community has for some time been considering the legal position in relation to contracts signed by customers at home. It seems likely that as a result, in years to come, there will be a general law introduced giving a general cooling off (i.e. cancellation) period to virtually all such customers making contracts of any real value.

Business Advertisements

A business may advertise in a way in which it is common for ordinary private individuals also to advertise. The most obvious of these ways is perhaps in the small advertisements in a local newspaper. It may be important to the reader of the advertisement to know whether the person advertising is in fact a private individual or someone running a business. The Business Advertisements (Disclosure) Order 1977 requires a business advertiser of goods to make it clear in the advertisement somehow (by its content, format, size, place of publication or some other way) that it is a business which is advertising.

Defamation

It is not uncommon for an advertisement to state that a certain famous person approves, likes, uses or recommends the product. The assumption (no doubt usually correct) on the reader's or viewer's part, is that the famous person has given his or her consent to this and, indeed, has been paid for doing so. In one case this assumption was erroneous. Mr. Tolley was a famous amateur golfer. Unknown to him, his likeness was used in an advertisement for Fry's chocolate with a bar of chocolate sticking from his pocket. He won his claim for libel (defamation) since the advertisement could easily be taken as meaning that he had accepted payment (i.e. contrary to his amateur status). The case highlights one of the risks of using in advertisements people who have not given their consent.

Trade Descriptions

One of the main controls on advertising is the Trade Descriptions Act 1968. It contains offences preventing anyone wrongly claiming to have supplied goods to the Queen (or to anyone else) or wrongly claiming royal approval, e.g. by displaying an emblem resembling the Queen's Award to Industry. It also allows the government to make regulations requiring specified information to be included in advertisements of specified goods. More importantly, it creates two general criminal offences, one relating to statements about goods and the other to statements about services.

Goods

Section 1 creates the criminal offence aimed at false descriptions of goods. The list of types of description which could be false is very long. It includes such things as the quantity, composition, method or date of manufacture, history and fitness for purpose of the goods. The offence catches a trader who applies a false trade description to goods. It also catches a trader, e.g. a retailer, who supplies goods to which a false trade description has already been attached. Suppose a shoe manufacturer wrongly labels a pair of shoes as 'all leather'. It is possible for both him and also the shopkeeper who later sells the shoes to be convicted – though, as we shall see a little later, the shopkeeper *may* have a defence.

Perhaps the type of trader most commonly caught is the second hand car dealer. One common way of him misdescribing the car is to leave the car in his showroom with a false odometer reading, i.e. with a mileage reading much lower than the number of miles actually covered by the car. It may be that the car dealer has himself 'clocked' the car, i.e. wound back the reading. He is still guilty if the 'clocking' was done by a previous owner. In this situation, however, (though not where he has himself done the 'clocking') the law allows the defence of a disclaimer. Thus he is not guilty if he has displayed (usually by sticking it on the dashboard) a notice which is sufficiently precise and compelling, to the effect that the odometer reading can not be relied upon as an accurate reflection of the mileage of the car.

The offence can be committed only where the false description is associated with the *supply or sale* of goods (or potential supply or sale of them). Thus a garage which after testing a customer's car gives an M.O.T. certificate (or refuses one) and in the process misdescribes the car, will not be guilty. Similarly, if when I collect my watch from the repairer, the repairer misdescribes the fault, he also will not be guilty of the offence.

On the other hand, the car dealer who is brought a car by a customer to see if the dealer will buy it and who lies saying the car is irreparable and fit only for scrap, will be guilty. His false statement was associated with the sale (or potential sale) of the goods, i.e. to himself.

One final point is that the accused can be guilty even though he did not know that the description in question was false. There are only limited defences available which will be explained after we have looked at false statements about services.

Services

Section 14 of the Act creates the offence concerned with false statements about services. Like the offence concerned with goods, it can be committed only by someone acting in the course of a business or profession. The offence is committed by making a false statement about 'services, accommodation or facilities'. The accused will be guilty if he knew the statement was false or alternatively if he was reckless in making the statement.

The type of person most commonly caught for the offence is the travel firm. A number of brochures have been found to contain false statements. In order for a conviction to be secured, it must be shown that there was a false statement of fact. It is not enough that a promise was made which was later broken, say, that a courier would be in attendance throughout the customer's stay. A promise, if broken, may well give the customer a right to damages for breach of contract. For a trader to be convicted under the Trade Descriptions Act, there must be a statement of fact which is false when made or read (i.e. before the holiday). An example might be 'The Majestic Hotel is only two minutes walk from the beach'.

There is a requirement that the accused, to be convicted, must have known the statement to be false or must have made it recklessly. This means that he must check his advertisement and take reasonable care to check its accuracy. Otherwise he will be reckless. It does not mean, however, that he must travel half way round the globe to check whether a detail he has been given about a hotel is true.

Although many of the cases involve travel firms, anyone whose business is supplying a service can be guilty, e.g. chimney sweeps, repairers, builders, plumbers, television rental companies. The list could be endless!

Defences

There are certain defences available to anyone charged with an offence under the Trade Descriptions Act. They are that the commission of the offence was due to one of the following: mistake, reliance on information supplied, act or default of another person, an accident or some other cause beyond the accused's control. However, none of these is a defence unless the accused can also show that he took all reasonable precautions and exercised all due diligence to avoid commission of the offence. The retailer of shoes incorrectly labelled by the manufacturer as 'all leather' might well have such a defence – but not, for example, if he had been informed of the misdescription and had subsequently failed to remove the labels from his remaining pairs. A car dealer who sells or displays a car which has previously been 'clocked' by someone else will not have a defence unless he has displayed a disclaimer. If he has not even taken that simple precaution, he has not taken *all* reasonable precautions to avoid committing the offence.

Where an accused pleads the defence that it was because of someone else's act or default, he must make available to the prosecution such information as he has about that other person. Then, if indeed it was the latter's act or default which caused the offence, he can be charged.

Enforcement and Sanctions

The Trade Descriptions Act is enforced by the trading standards departments of local authorities. Proceedings can be brought against the offender in the Magistrates' Court where, if convicted, he can be fined up to a maximum of £2,000. In the rare case of a trial on indictment (i.e. in a Crown Court, before a judge and jury), the maximum fine is unlimited and a sentence of imprisonment (maximum two years) is even possible.

An important point is that the criminal court can, at the same time as passing sentence, make a compensation order. This is an order requiring the accused to pay the victim compensation. The maximum amount of a compensation order on any one conviction is £2,000 in the Magistrates' Court and unlimited in the Crown Court. It should be noted that with a holiday brochure containing a false trade description, a separate offence is committed every time it is read! The same would presumably be true of a newspaper advertisement or a poster advertisement. Even if the advertiser has been convicted once, it is therefore quite possible for further charges to be brought the sole purpose of which is to secure a compensation order for another victim.

Prices

There is an offence in the Trade Descriptions Act concerned with misleading price information. This is about to be swept away and replaced by provisions in the Consumer Protection Act 1987 which is expected to be brought into force during 1988.

The Consumer Protection Act 1987

We have already seen in Chapter 8 that the Consumer Protection Act creates a general duty not to market unsafe products.

It also contains separate provisions on misleading price indications. It will make it an offence for any trader to give consumers a misleading price indication about any goods, services, accomodation or facilities. There will be issued a Code of Practice giving practical guidance. The Code is likely to cover such things as: price comparisons with the trader's own previous prices; comparisons with other traders' prices; comparisons with a recommended price or other suggested price; price reductions, introductory offers, statements that prices are pegged for a limited time or likely to rise soon, statements about V.A.T.; service charges (e.g. in restaurants); call out charges; holiday prices; bureaux de change services; sales of new homes. Before the Act is brought into force the Code of Practice will be available from the Department of Trade and Industry, 1–19 Victoria Street, London, SW1H OET.

13   Credit Law

Many credit transactions are regulated by the Consumer Credit Act 1974. The Act is a piece of consumer protection and its provisions are designed to protect the person to whom credit is given, i.e. the debtor. Most traders will, in the course of their businesses, both give and receive credit. The Consumer Credit Act does not, however, apply to all credit transactions. Its protection is limited to those debtors who might loosely be termed ordinary consumers. These will in some cases include traders, because the Act generally applies where (i) the amount of credit does not exceed £15,000, and (ii) the debtor (consumer) is not a limited company.

No doubt a trader who is given credit would like to know whether the transaction is subject to the Act, so he can thereby discover whether he has the protection given by the Act. A trader who is giving credit has a more compelling reason to know whether that credit is subject to the Act. He needs to ensure that he does not break the law laid down by the Act. Where a credit agreement is subject to the Act, the Act imposes numerous requirements upon the person who gives the credit. He must be licensed; his credit advertisements and quotations must comply with certain regulations; any percentage rate quoted must be calculated in a certain way (i.e. as the A.P.R.); the agreement must be contained in a document of a certain type of which a copy (sometimes two copies) must be given to the debtor etc. There are risks and penalties for any trader who fails to comply with these and other requirements.

A trader might at this stage be thinking that he would prefer not to give credit rather than to have to bother with the Consumer Credit Act. There are, however, two problems with that. First, if he does not offer any credit facilities at all to his customers, his turnover may well suffer. Secondly, if he adopts the technique of not himself offering credit but instead directing his customers to a separate source of finance, he may well find himself still in some measure subject to the Consumer Credit Act. This is because he will thereby be casting himself in the role of a credit-broker and credit-brokers are required by the Act to be licensed.

Before looking at the duties placed upon traders affected by the Act, we shall first examine more closely the range of transactions caught by the Act. A warning must also be given. It is that the Act is detailed and complicated and what follows in this chapter is only as accurate as a short account can be. Free guidance literature for traders is available from the Office of Fair Trading, Field House, Bream's Buildings, London EC4A 1PR.

Range of Transactions Caught by the Consumer Credit Act

Consumer Credit Agreements

With four exceptions, the Act regulates all credit agreements. Regulated agreements are called consumer credit agreements. The four exceptions are:

1 an agreement where the person receiving the credit (i.e. the debtor) is a corporate body
2 an agreement for fixed sum credit where the amount of the credit exceeds £15,000
3 an agreement for running-amount credit where the credit limit exceeds £15,000

4 an agreement declared exempt by the Act.

The first of these exceptions means that where a company is given credit, the agreement can not be subject to the Act. On the other hand a sole trader or partnership could well be a debtor under a regulated agreement. The second exception deals with 'fixed sum' credit agreements. These are agreements where it is agreed at the outset the exact amount of credit to be taken by the debtor (e.g. a loan of £10,000). If the amount exceeds £15,000 the agreement is not caught by the Act. For this purpose the important figure is the amount of the *credit*, i.e. not including the interest or other charges which the debtor must also pay. Thus a loan of £14,000 to a man for a year at a rate of ten per cent will involve him in repaying £15,400 at the end of the year. Nevertheless, it is still a regulated agreement because the amount of the *credit* (£14,000) does not exceed £15,000.

The third exception deals with 'running-account' credit. That is a situation where the actual amount of credit which will be used is not fixed at the outset, i.e. where the debtor is free to use or not use the credit as he wishes (usually up to a maximum credit limit at any one time). An easy example is of a bank overdraft agreement where the debtor is given permission to overdraw. He may or may not actually do so. These are termed 'running-account' because usually the debtor has the ability to take credit, pay it back (wholly or partly), take it again, pay it off again and so on. If the credit limit is both realistic and also in excess of £15,000 the agreement is not regulated by the Consumer Credit Act. A credit limit is realistic if its full amount is likely at some time to be needed by the debtor. In the following cases, however, the fact that a credit limit is above £15,000 will be irrelevant: (i) if it is unlikely that the debtor will ever need a limit over

£15,000; (ii) if he is unable to draw more than £15,000 on any one occasion; (iii) if the terms become more onerous for the debtor (e.g. he pays a higher rate of interest) on him going over £15,000 (or some lower figure). In each of these three cases the agreements will be regulated by the Act even though the credit limit exceeds £15,000.

So far, then, a credit agreement where the debtor is an individual or a partnership and which is within the £15,000 limit will be regulated by the Act. These will include all sorts of credit agreements: credit-sale, hire-purchase, overdraft, loan, credit card, shop 'budget' accounts etc.

Exempt Agreements

The Act, however, declares certain agreements exempt. There are three main categories of exempt agreement. The most important of these is the 'general trade debt' exemption. This describes the situation which is commonplace in ordinary everyday trade, namely a 'one-off' situation where goods or services are provided and the customer is to pay for them later. Usually, of course, the bill is payable within a short time afterwards (e.g. within thirty days) and is expected, when it is paid, to be paid in full. Under the Act such credit agreements are exempt. They are exempt provided the credit has to be paid in four or fewer instalments. The general trade exemption also covers goods or services which are supplied on a regular or continuing basis to be paid for periodically (i.e. a running account).

Typical examples would be household milk and newspaper deliveries. Here there is a credit agreement, since the goods are obtained first and paid for later. Such agreements are exempt, however, if the arrangement is that each periodical bill is to be settled in full by a single payment. Thus household milk and newspaper delivery agreements are exempt. For the same reason so are certain credit card agreements. These are those credit card agreements, such as Diners Club and American Express, which require each periodical bill to be paid in full by a single payment. Such cards are different from credit cards where the card holder is allowed extended credit which he can, if he wishes, pay off gradually in instalments. Cards of this latter type – e.g, Access, Visa and a number of store cards such as the Marks & Spencer Chargecard – are regulated by the Act.

The second main category of exempt agreement is the 'low cost credit' exemption. Credit (usually a straight loan) not tied to any particular use will be exempt if the charge (i.e. interest and other amounts charged) is sufficiently low. It will be sufficiently low if *either* it does not exceed thirteen per cent (calculated according to a stipulated formula) *or* it does not exceed by more than one per cent the base rates charged by the main British banks. In fact, someone granting credit at such a low rate as to be within the exemption, will almost certainly be doing so at a loss. It is likely therefore that only those free or cheap loans given as fringe benefits by employers to their employees are likely to qualify for this exemption.

The third main category of exempt agreements are house purchase, land mortgage loans granted by building societies, local authorities and certain other bodies including a number of insurance companies, friendly societies, trade unions and charities. Certain agreements providing credit to be used in connection with overseas trade are also exempt.

Consumer Hire Agreements

Surprisingly, the Consumer Credit Act regulates not only credit agreements but also certain hire agreements.

A hire-purchase agreement is in any case regulated as being a type of credit agreement. Any other agreement to hire goods will also be regulated if it has all the following three features:

- the hirer is an individual or a partnership (i.e. not a company)
- the agreement is capable of lasting more than three calendar months
- the agreement does not require payments which together total more than £15,000.

Thus the average TV hire agreement will be regulated by the Act. Similarly a car hire agreement (unless it is agreed to be for three months or less) will be regulated if the hirer is an individual or partnership.

Licensing Requirements

Anyone carrying on one of the following categories of business must be licensed to do so. He must be licensed even if that is not the main part, or even a large part, of his business. If in his business he carries on these activities he must be licensed:

Category	Business
A	Consumer Credit
B	Consumer Hire
C	Credit Brokerage
D	Debt-adjusting and debt-counselling
E	Debt collecting
F	Credit Reference Agency

Licences are issued by the Director General of Fair Trading and forms etc. are obtainable from the Office of Fair Trading, Consumer Credit Licensing Branch,

Government Buildings, Bromyard Avenue, Acton, London W3 7BB.

Category A includes any business which grants credit under regulated agreements and Category B, any business which lends out goods on hire under regulated consumer hire agreements. Credit brokers require a licence under Category C. A credit broker is anyone who in the course of his business introduces would-be customers to a consumer credit business or consumer hire business. A lot of apparently ordinary businesses selling goods or services qualify as credit brokers. The sorts of thing involved include cars, photocopiers, dentists' chairs, double glazing, central heating, coffee vending machines, house extensions, garden landscaping – even electronic shrines sold to clergymen! The point is that the person selling the goods (we will call him the dealer) will often have an arrangement with a given source of credit, a finance house. The arrangement is that the dealer will refer to the finance house any potential buyer (customer) who wishes to have finance (i.e. credit) in order to buy the goods. The finance house will then make a credit agreement to give credit to the customer so as to enable him to buy the dealer's goods or services. If the dealer does have this sort of arrangement he needs to be licensed as a credit broker. Sometimes the finance house will make a straight loan to the customer. Sometimes the arrangement will be, instead, that it buys the goods for cash from the dealer and will itself agree to supply the same goods (either on credit terms or on hire) to the customer. Either way, the dealer who introduced the customer to the finance house needs to be licensed as a credit broker.

The remaining categories do not require a lot of explanation. Debt-adjusters and counsellors are people who by way of business give advice or help to debtors about settling up consumer credit or consumer hire debts.

Their services are usually sought by debtors who are in financial difficulties. Debt-collecting is self explanatory. Credit Reference Agencies are those agencies which collect information about the creditworthiness of individuals for the purpose of issuing that information (usually in return for a fee) to interested parties. A credit grantor, before agreeing to advance credit will often pay a credit reference agency for a report on the would-be customer.

Fit Person

A licence can be refused or withdrawn from any person who is not fit to have a licence. A person (or company) may be found not to be fit if he or any of his employees or agents have done any of the following things:

(i) committed an offence of fraud, dishonesty or violence
(ii) broken any law relating to credit
(iii) practised sexual or colour (or racial or ethnic) discrimination
(iv) engaged in business practices which are deceitful, oppressive, unfair or improper.

Sanctions

It is a criminal offence for anyone to engage in an activity for which he should be licensed when he does not have the appropriate licence. The consequences of unlicensed trading can be much more than that. A business granting credit is unable to enforce against the customer any regulated credit or hire agreement which was made when the business was unlicensed. This means that the business has no legal right to succeed in recovering repayments due to it under regulated agreements made by it when it was unlicensed. The position can be even worse than that because even if the business granting credit was licensed, it will be unable to enforce agreements resulting from introduction by an unlicensed credit broker. Thus it behoves any credit granting business considering accepting an introduction of a customer to check that the trader making the introduction does have a current credit-broker's (Category C) licence. This can be done (for a small fee) by a search of the Consumer Credit Public Register (Office of Fair Trading, Government Buildings, Bromyard Avenue, Acton, London W3 7BB).

In the event that because of unlicensed trading, a credit granting business finds itself with some (or, more usually, a lot of) unenforceable agreements, an application can be made to the Director General of Fair Trading to allow the agreements to be enforced. No doubt the Director General will not oblige without both hearing any excuses there are for the unlicensed trading and also considering whether the unlicensed trader was a fit person to be licensed anyway.

Canvassing

The Consumer Credit Act has curbed the practice of door to door peddling of credit, i.e. of a representative calling at private residences with a view to getting someone there to take credit or to take goods on hire. The curbs are twofold. First there is a total ban on such canvassing where the credit being promoted is not connected with any particular goods or services, i.e. the canvassing of straight ordinary cash loans is a criminal offence. On the other hand there is not a total ban on the doorstep selling of goods and services on credit. Thus the double glazing or central heating salesman is not prohibited from seeking to persuade customers to acquire his merchandise on credit. That is so even if the credit suggested is a loan to enable the customer to buy that merchandise. This sort of canvassing is allowed provided that the person is operating under a licence (see above) which specifically authorises canvassing off trade premises. Of course, the individual salesman does not need to be licensed, but rather the firm for whom he works. If he is employed by a double glazing firm which will introduce its customers to another firm (the credit grantor) for finance, then the double glazing firm will need a category C (credit broker's) licence which specifically authorises canvassing off trade premises. Otherwise the door to door canvassing will amount to unlicensed trading with the risk of the sanctions mentioned earlier.

There is no restriction on canvassing by visiting *trade* premises in order to persuade people to become customers by taking credit or goods on hire.

Advertisements and Quotations

Credit and hire advertisements must not be misleading and have to comply with regulations, as also does any quotation given for a potential regulated agreement. Most significant in the regulations is the requirement that whenever a rate of charge (or rate of interest) is shown, the A.P.R. must be shown. The A.P.R. is the true Annual Percentage Rate of charge calculated in the way laid down in the regulations. This is to try to ensure that members of the public are able to compare A.P.R.'s and get an accurate idea of whose rate is truly the lowest.

Other Controls on Seeking Business

Children

It is a criminal offence to send or give to someone under eighteen a circular inviting him to obtain credit or goods on hire (or inviting him to seek further information about it).

Unsolicited Credit Tokens

The commonest type of credit token is a credit card. It is a criminal offence to issue a credit token to someone who has not asked for it, though there is an exception allowed in the case of renewal or replacement credit tokens.

Credit-broker's Fees

Some credit-brokers will charge a customer a fee for introducing that customer to a business which provides credit (or goods on hire). The Consumer Credit Act prevents the credit-broker being entitled to any more than £3 for an unsuccessful introduction (i.e. if after six months the customer has not got the credit or goods on hire). If the customer has already paid more than that, he is entitled to recover the excess over the £3.

Credit Reference Agencies

A customer who applies for credit (or goods on hire) is entitled to discover from the firm to which he applied, the name and address of any credit reference agency which was consulted about the customer's creditworthiness. Any individual (and it might well be someone whose application for credit has been refused) is entitled for a fee of £1 to make a written request of any credit reference agency for a copy of its file on him. If he considers the file inaccurate he can require a change or the addition to the file of his own note (of not more than 200 words). If the credit reference agency refuses, the individual can appeal to the Director General of Fair Trading.

Documentation of Agreements

With only a few exceptions, regulated consumer credit and consumer hire agreements must be made in such a way that they comply with the documentation requirements of the Consumer Credit Act. If they do not, the business which provided the credit or the goods on hire will find it difficult or impossible to enforce the agreement. That is, it may be unable to enforce repayment of the debt.

The main exceptions where the agreement does not have to comply with the requirements are: bank overdraft agreements; certain small value agreements involving credit of £50 to be used for a specific purpose; certain agreements to finance payments arising out of a death (e.g. payment of inheritance tax).

Form and Content

The Act lays down requirements as to the form and contents of the written agreement. The agreement will thus be legible and will acquaint the customer with his legal rights.

Signature

The agreement must be signed by the customer in person as well as by or on behalf of the business providing the credit (or goods on hire).

Copies

The customer must be given a copy of the document so that after he has himself signed the agreement he is left with a copy of what he has signed. It may be that what he has signed is only a proposed agreement, i.e. that it will not be signed until later on behalf of the business providing the credit. If so, then after the latter signature, another copy (this time of the agreement as signed by both sides) must be received by the customer within seven days following the making of the agreement.

Variation of an Agreement

If the customer and the person who granted the credit agree to vary the agreement, then documentation requirements apply which are similar to those which apply when the agreement is first made.

Customer's Rights of Cancellation

We have seen that there are controls on the door to door peddling of credit (see Canvassing, page 166 above). We saw that there is no control of such canvassing at premises where a business is carried on. Also we saw that if there is specific authorisation in the relevant licence, it is permitted to canvass even at private residences to sell specific items (e.g. double glazing, encyclopaedias, central heating) making credit available.

Here, however, we discover that, although such canvassing is permitted, any credit agreement which the customer signs as a result of the canvassing is likely to be cancellable. This is because a regulated agreement (with a few exceptions) is cancellable if two conditions are satisfied:

(i) the antecedent negotiations included oral representations in the presence of the customer (i.e. the door to door salesman spoke to him)

(ii) the customer signed the agreement other than at the trade premises of the salesman, the salesman's firm or the business granting the credit (e.g. the customer signed at his own premises, whether his private or business premises).

The customer's right of cancellation must be clearly spelt out on the contract he signs and on each copy he is given. He has a cooling off period during which he is entitled to cancel by simply serving (or posting) a written note to that effect. The period will last at least five days and often longer. The effect of cancellation is, roughly, that the agreement is undone. If the customer has received any goods, he must return them but is entitled to recover any payments he has made.

Misuse of Credit Facilities

As a general rule the customer can not be made liable when someone else makes unauthorised use of the credit facilities. However, in the common case where a credit card is stolen, the customer can be made liable up to a maximum of £50 for such loss.

Security

There is no room here to detail all the law on various forms of security e.g. mortgages, pawn, the right to repossess a hire purchase item, guarantees and indemnities.

It should certainly be pointed out, however, that anyone granting credit to a person under eighteen ought seriously to consider taking some guarantee or indemnity from some credit worthy adult. Otherwise he may find himself not legally entitled to enforce the agreement.

Enforcement of Regulated Agreements

Sometimes a credit agreement will provide for the creditor to have the right to do certain rather drastic things if the customer falls into arrears. It may be that the agreement has an 'accelerated payments' clause, which states that the creditor can demand immediate payment of all the outstanding payments (i.e. even of those for which the due dates have not yet passed). In the case of a hire-purchase agreement, the agreement may contain a 'termination' clause giving the creditor the right to terminate the whole agreement (i.e. to recover the goods). Both these things could be drastic for the customer. If a customer has already fallen behind with one or more instalments he is hardly likely to be able immediately to pay off all the others as well. A termination clause in a hire purchase agreement could result in the customer having the goods repossessed when he is within only one or two instalments of completing his payments.

The Consumer Credit Act gives the customer certain protections. First, the creditor must serve a written default notice on the customer before he activates a termination clause or accelerated payments clause. This will give the customer at least seven days notice. Secondly, after the seven days, the Act prohibits the creditor from simply seizing the hire-purchase goods (i.e. provided the customer has paid at least one third of the total price). This means that the creditor must go to court in order to claim accelerated payments or to recover possession of the goods. In these court proceedings the customer can apply for a 'time order'. If the court grants that request, it effectively gives the customer another chance. It can spread back out over a period of time the money claimed as accelerated. It can effectively re-jig the repayment pattern so as to make it easier for the customer to complete the payments. Of course, if the customer fails to keep up with the payments ordered by the court, the creditor could always return to court and ask for immediate accelerated payment of the lot or for return of the goods (whichever the case may be).

Connected Lender Liability

Before leaving the topic of consumer credit, reference must be made back to section 75 of the Consumer Credit Act whereby a creditor (usually a finance company) can be made liable for breaches of contract and misrepresentation by a supplier of goods or services. This can occur where there are arrangements between the supplier and the creditor as often occurs with credit cards and with double glazing and central heating installers. If there are these arrangements, *and* the credit agreement is regulated by the Consumer Credit Act *and* the cash price of the item in question was over £100, the creditor (the finance company) is liable together with the supplier (see pages 119 and 130 above).

Part Three
The Business as
Employer

14 The Nature of Employment Law

Employment law governs the relationship between employers and workers. In this book we look mainly at the relationship between employers and individual workers. We explain how the law regulates this relationship and the duties which the law imposes on employers.

The law also regulates the relationship between employers and trade unions. The final two chapters outline the rights and obligations of employers in their dealings with trade unions.

In this chapter we look at the sources of employment law and the machinery for resolving disputes over workers' rights.

The Role of Contract and the Civil Courts

The employment relationship is based on contract. Whenever one person agrees to do work for another for payment there is a contract between them. At its most basic, this contract will specify the job which the worker has agreed to do and the wage he or she will receive for doing it. Most contracts concerning employment will contain many more terms. They may, for example, state that the worker must do a certain amount of overtime or stipulate holiday and sick pay entitlement. They may state that a given period of notice is required to end the relationship. They may give the employer the right to move the worker to another job. The sources of contractual terms are examined in detail in Chapter 16.

Employment contracts, like any other contracts, can be enforced in the ordinary civil courts. If one party alleges that the other has breached the contract, he or she can seek a remedy in the County Court or the High Court, depending on the size of the claim. (The County Court deals with claims for £5,000 or less.) The ordinary courts also deal with claims in tort arising out of the employment relationship. A worker may be injured at work and sue the employer. An employer may seek a remedy against a trade union threatening unlawful industrial action. The procedures for enforcing these claims are in general the same as those for enforcing claims arising in any other context.

The Role of Legislation

As well as rights arising under their contracts, workers are also given many rights by legislation. These rights include the right not to be discriminated against on grounds of sex or race; the right not to be unfairly dismissed; rights to certain payments and to time off from work; and the right to a minimum notice period. Not all these rights apply to all workers; some are given only to 'employees'. The definition of an 'employee' is explored in Chapter 15. Some rights also require a minimum period of 'continuous employment', a concept explained in Chapter 17. In some cases the law lays down only a minimum 'floor' and employees may be given more generous rights by their contracts. This applies, for example, to payments when laid off and to notice periods. In this situation, the more generous contractual right prevails. Employers cannot, however, force their workers to surrender or reduce their statutory rights. Any agreement which attempted to do this would be void.

In some areas, such as discipline, health and safety, and sex and race discrimination, Codes of Practice have been issued. These give advice as to how to comply with the law. Breach of one of these Codes does not of itself mean that an employer has acted unlawfully, but the Code is admissible in evidence in any legal proceedings.

Industrial Tribunals

Claims to enforce those individual employment rights which are derived from legislation are dealt with by a specialist system of labour courts known as industrial tribunals. Industrial tribunals consist of a legally qualified chairperson and two lay members with industrial experience. The lay members are taken from two panels appointed by the Secretary of State for Employment, one after consultation with trade unions and one after consultation with employers' organisations. All three tribunal members have an equal vote in deciding cases but the vast majority of decisions are unanimous. There are three Central Offices of Industrial Tribunals; one in London, one in Glasgow and one in Belfast. Tribunals sit in a number of centres around the country.

Industrial tribunals are intended to provide an easily accessible, informal, cheap and speedy method of settling employment disputes. An individual worker can begin tribunal proceedings by filling in a simple standard form which is available from job centres and unemployment benefit offices. This form must be sent to the appropriate Central Office, which then sends a copy to the employer against whom the complaint is being made. The employer has fourteen days in which to indicate whether or not he or she is resisting the claim and, if so, on what ground. Tribunals can order either party to disclose further particulars of their case where appropriate. They can also order, on the application of either party, the production of documents by the other side either before or at the hearing. Witnesses can be ordered to attend tribunal hearings.

It was originally intended that parties appearing before industrial tribunals would not, in general, have legal representation. Either side may represent themselves or, unlike in the ordinary courts, be represented by any other person. Workers are sometimes represented by trade union officials. The procedure is designed for the layperson to use. The normal rules of evidence and court etiquette do not apply, and the chairperson can help the unrepresented party to present his or her case by asking appropriate questions. In 1983, some forty per cent of employers and thirty seven per cent of workers appeared in person. It has become increasingly common for parties to have legal representation, however. In 1983, forty nine per cent of employers and thirty seven per cent of workers had legal representatives at the hearing. Legal aid is not available for tribunal proceedings, although persons of limited means can obtain up to £40 worth of free legal advice from a solicitor. Usually each side will bear its own costs. A party is only ordered to pay the costs of the other side if they are judged to have acted frivolously, vexatiously or otherwise unreasonably. Tribunals have power to hold a 'pre-hearing assessment' to 'weed out' unmeritorious claims or defences. A party who pursues a case after being warned that their argument is unmeritorious risks costs being awarded against them if they lose.

An employer who is on the receiving end of a complaint may wish to try to settle it before it reaches the industrial tribunal. This will save management time in attending the hearing and legal costs if lawyers are involved. Clearly an employer who offers a worker a payment to settle will want this to be conditional on the worker dropping the case. Such an agreement will bind the worker only if it is reached with the assistance of an A.C.A.S. Conciliation Officer. A.C.A.S. (the Advisory, Conciliation and Arbitration Service) is an independent body which has the general function of improving industrial relations. A.C.A.S. Conciliation Officers are sent copies of complaints presented to industrial tribunals. They are then required to try to promote a settlement at the request of both parties or on their own initiative if they think they have a reasonable prospect of success in achieving this. If the parties reach a settlement themselves, they must call in a Conciliation Officer to make this settlement valid. If the case later goes to a tribunal, nothing said to the Conciliation Officer is admissible in evidence without the consent of the person who said it.

Most cases are heard by tribunals within sixteen weeks of an application being made. This compares with many months, or even years, for cases in the ordinary courts. Statutory claims are required to be presented to tribunals within a specified period of the act complained of. The commonest period is three months; this is the time limit for unfair dismissal claims, for example. There is generally a discretion for the tribunal to extend this period where it was not 'reasonably practicable' for the complainant to comply with the time limit. The circumstances in which this discretion can be exercised are limited. Illness or other physical obstacles would count; merely making a mistake, or acting on a skilled advisor's mistake, would not.

A party who considers that an industrial tribunal made a mistake as to the law in deciding his or her case may appeal to the Employment Appeal Tribunal (E.A.T.). There is, in general, no scope to appeal against a tribunal's finding of fact. The E.A.T. consists of a judge and two or four lay members, again selected for their industrial relations experience. Further appeals can be made, with leave of a court, to the Court of Appeal and the House of Lords. Most appeals do not go beyond the E.A.T.

The Relationship Between Courts and Industrial Tribunals

The division of jurisdiction between the ordinary courts and the industrial tribunals in dealing with employment matters can seem unnecessarily complicating. This is particularly so in the area of dismissals. If a worker is dismissed without receiving the contractual period of notice, he or she will have a claim for breach of contract in the ordinary courts. The worker may also wish to claim the dismissal was unfair, a matter for a tribunal to decide. In practice, however, if the worker is successful at tribunal proceedings the compensation awarded there will often cover the loss caused by the breach of contract.

15 The Structure and Composition of the Workforce

One of the first questions which anyone starting a business needs to decide is how many people to employ and upon what terms. Should they be 'on the books' or self-employed? Should they be paid a regular wage or paid by the job? Should they be temporary or permanent? Should they be full-time or part-time? The answers to these questions will depend upon the nature and needs of the business. The first part of this chapter explains the relevance of these answers in deciding a worker's employment status and the legal resons why this status matters.

The ways in which employers choose their workers will also vary according to the nature of their business. In relation to recruitment and promotion the law provides that employers must not discriminate on grounds of sex or race. There are also provisions relating to the employment of trade union members, disabled persons and persons with a criminal record. In the second half of the chapter we look at how employers can ensure that they comply with these provisions.

The Legal Classification of Employment Relationships

People may do work for each other under a variety of contractual arrangements. The law makes a basic distinction between, on the one hand, workers who are employees, and who work under a contract of employment (or service), and, on the other hand, self-employed workers. Where a self-employed person undertakes to perform work personally, and cannot delegate it to another, he or she will usually work under a 'contract for services'. Contracts may take other forms as well; for example, where the only obligation is to purchase a finished work, such as a picture or a play, the result may be a contract of sale. In the context of employment law, however, the crucial issue normally is whether the contract is, or is not, a contract of employment. If it is not, its exact classification is usually irrelevant.

The consequences of being an employee

The classification of a worker as an 'employee' has several important consequences:

1 Most employment rights apply only to employees. These include the right to complain of unfair dismissal, to claim statutory redundancy payments, guarantee pay and time off rights, and the right to a written statement of employment terms. (Capacity to claim these rights generally requires a certain period of 'continuous employment', a concept discussed in Chapter 17.) Some employment rights, however, apply also to those employed under a contract personally to execute any work or labour. These include the right not to be discriminated against on grounds of sex or race and the right to have deductions from wages made only in accordance with the Wages Act 1986.
2 Income tax payable by employees is deducted at source by employers on a Pay As You Earn basis. The self-employed pay their own tax in arrears.

3 Employees are liable for Class 1 social security contributions, part of which is paid by their employer. The self-employed pay their own contributions, at a lower rate. Only employees can claim unemployment benefit.

4 Employers are vicariously liable to third parties for torts committed by their employees in the course of their employment. That means that they, as well as or instead of the employee, can be sued for damages. Employers should, of course, seek to insure themselves against such risks. (In some cases, such as injuries caused to fellow employees and road traffic accidents, insurance is compulsory.) Employers are not, in general, liable for torts committed by the self-employed.

5 Some industrial safety legislation applies only to employees and they are owed higher duties than the self-employed under the Health and Safety at Work etc. Act 1974 (see Chapter 20). The standard of care owed at common law to employees is also higher.

6 If an employer goes bankrupt, employees, but not the self-employed, are preferred creditors in respect of any wages owed to them for the preceding four months, up to a maximum of £800.

When is a worker an employee?

Whether or not a worker is an 'employee' depends on the attributes of the employment relationship. Perhaps surprisingly, given its importance, there is no statutory definition of the term 'employee'. It has been left to the courts to formulate tests for distinguishing between employees and other types of worker. One point should be made clear at the start. The parties cannot decide the legal classification of their relationship simply by putting a 'label' on it. Employers and workers may be tempted to classify their relationship as self-employment for tax and social security reasons. If, however, this classification is challenged by the Inland Revenue or DHSS, or by the worker later wanting to claim employment protection rights, the courts and tribunals will look at all the facts to determine a worker's true classification. Only in rare cases of true ambiguity will the 'label' decide the issue. (To deal with problems of tax evasion in the building industry, the Finance Act 1979 provides that builders who employ sub-contractors must deduct thirty per cent of the labour cost to pay in tax unless the sub-contractor has a tax exemption certificate.)

Most people have some idea about who is an employee and who is self-employed. The person who works a regular thirty-five hour week for one employer for a fixed wage would be generally regarded as an employee. By contrast, the plumber or architect who does one-off jobs for a variety of people would be seen as self-employed. Not all situations are so clear-cut, however. A person may work half the week for one employer and the remainder of the time for several people. Their remuneration may be based upon the amount of business which comes in. They may work only when the employer needs them and it suits them so to do. The variety of arrangements under which people may work for others makes it crucial to consider the factors which indicate 'employee' status.

At one time the courts placed great emphasis on the extent of an employer's control over a worker. If the employer could tell the worker not only what work to do but also how to do it, the worker was an employee. In the case of unskilled workers this test can often provide a definitive answer but it is less suited to situations where the worker has specialised skills and training. A later test was to look at whether the worker was an integral part of the employer's business or only accessory to it. Under this test, a full-time writer for a magazine would be an employee, an occasional contributor who writes for a number of publications would not be. This test, too, has its limitations, however, and the tendency now is to look at all the features of the relationship, including control. One factor of particular importance is whether the worker can be seen as an entrepreneur, running his own business. If so, he will be self-employed. Whether the worker takes a risk on making a profit in doing a job will be highly relevant here. Whether or not he invests in his own equipment is also material. Previous practice in relation to tax and social security contributions and the parties' intentions will also be looked at although, as previously indicated, these factors are in no way conclusive. The tribunals and courts conduct a wide-ranging 'weighing-up' exercise to decide the issue.

Exclusive service for one employer is a factor which points towards employee status. Nevertheless, a person may still be an employee if he or she works part-time on a regular basis for an employer, even if the rest of the time is spent working for another or others. This will depend on the other terms of the relationship. In one case, for example, a part-time interviewer for a market research company was held to be an employee, even though her only obligation was to complete a particular survey within a specified period. She did not provide any equipment or risk any capital and had to follow strict procedures when conducting interviews. However, employee status does require both sides to be subject to some degree of obligation. This excludes entirely 'casual' work. If a worker has no obligation to accept work when it is offered on any given occasion, and the employer has no obligation to provide it, the worker is not an employee. Having said that, mutual obligations may be inferred from a course of dealing over time. In one case, two women had worked at home for a clothing manufacturer for over four years.

The employers supplied their sewing machines. Although they could determine their own hours and take time off as they chose, in practice they had always worked whenever they were needed. The employers tried to share out the available work fairly. The court found that the conduct of the relationship (in practice) showed sufficient obligations on both sides to make the women employees. As this case also indicates, home-workers, as well as those who work on their employers' premises, may be classed as employees, depending on the circumstances.

Employers may decide to obtain labour, usually on a temporary basis, through an employment agency or business. Workers thus supplied probably have no contractual relationship with the hirer at all. Fee-charging employment agencies and businesses require a licence under the Employment Agencies Act 1973.

In the majority of cases, the appropriate employment classification for a particular worker will be clear. In less obvious cases, employers should decide the basis of employment in the light of the considerations outlined above. Where the factors are evenly balanced, this may come down ultimately to a question of 'feel'.

Recruitment and Promotion: The Anti-Discrimination Legislation

Sex and Race Discrimination

The Sex Discrimination Act 1975 and the Race Relations Act 1976 make it unlawful for employers to discriminate against workers because of their sex or race, or because they are married, when they are choosing whom to employ. This involves looking at where job advertisements are placed, and what they say, as well as the final selection process. Employers must also avoid discriminating against persons on these grounds once they are in employment. They must not deny workers access to promotion, training, or other benefits, or choose workers for dismissal, because of their sex or race. It is also unlawful to pay workers less because of their race or give them other less favourable contractual terms than other groups. Giving workers less favourable contractual terms on grounds of sex is also unlawful, but this is dealt with by the equal pay legislation, discussed in Chapter 18. Unlike much employment protection legislation, the anti-discrimination legislation protects those who work under contracts for services as well as employees. Workers supplied by a third party, such as an employment agency, are also protected against discrimination by hiring employers. The legislation does not apply to employment where the work is done wholly or mainly outside Great Britain.

A worker who feels the victim of discrimination can complain to an industrial tribunal. If it upholds the complaint, the tribunal can order the employer to pay the worker compensation. The current maximum is £8,000. It can also recommend that the employer takes action to remove or reduce the adverse effect of the discrimination on the victim. The compensation awarded may be increased if the employer fails to take this action without reasonable justification. The Equal Opportunities Commission (E.O.C.) and Commission for Racial Equality (C.R.E.), which are independent bodies responsible for eliminating discrimination in their respective fields, may assist individuals to bring proceedings. They can also bring proceedings against persons who instruct or pressurise others to discriminate and in respect of discriminatory advertisements, as well as having broader investigative and educational functions. Both Commissions have issued Codes of

Practice which give guidance on how to comply with the legislation.

The main target of the Sex Discrimination Act is discrimination against women but it applies equally to discrimination against men. Special treatment afforded to women in connection with pregnancy or childbirth is excluded. However, it is unlawful to discriminate against a woman because she is pregnant where a man who needed time off work or other similar concessions would not be so treated. (As discussed in Chapter 19, it is also unfair to dismiss a woman because she is pregnant except in special circumstances.) Subjecting a person to unwanted sexual attention at work ('sexual harassment') can also amount to sex discrimination. In addition, the Sex Discrimination Act prohibits discrimination against, but not in favour of, married people.

The Race Relations Act prohibits discrimination on grounds of 'colour, race, nationality or ethnic or national origins'. Religion is not specifically covered but particular religious sects may constitute an ethnic group if they have a sufficiently distinctive cultural identity. Sikhs and Jews come into this category. Discrimination on religious grounds may also amount to indirect discrimination against persons of a particular race (see below).

It is also unlawful under both Acts to discriminate against persons because they bring proceedings under them or assist others to do so. This protection does not apply to a person whose allegation of discrimination was false and not made in good faith.

Unlawful discrimination may be direct or indirect. Direct discrimination means treating a person less favourably on grounds of his or her sex or race, or married status, than a person of a different sex or race, or an unmarried person, would be treated. Segregation on racial grounds amounts to less favourable treatment. So does discrimination against persons because they refuse to obey an employer's instruction to discriminate against others. (Giving such an instruction is in itself unlawful.) There was a breach of the Race Relations Act when a worker was dismissed because he refused to implement the employer's policy of excluding blacks from the premises.

Clearly refusing someone a job because of his or her sex or race is covered by direct discrimination. Discriminating against someone because of an assumption that his or her sex or race has particular characteristics is also covered. In one case the employers refused a woman training leave because they believed that, as her husband was working elsewhere, she would not return to her job. They acted on the stereotyped assumption that married women follow their husbands' jobs. This amounted to sex discrimination. Assuming that women are unreliable employees or less mobile or physically strong than men would amount to sex discrimination for similar reasons. Employers should always investigate the ability of each individual applicant to do a job on his or her own merits. There are specific situations where the legislation does allow employers to specify that they want a man or a woman. These include situations where there are considerations of privacy or decency involved or the provision of welfare or educational services. Authenticity in dramatic performances and other entertainments is also covered. The Race Relations Act also allows race to be specified in a very narrow range of circumstances. These include reasons of authenticity where an establishment serves food or drink, such as a Chinese or Indian restaurant. Also the Race Relations Act does not cover employment for the purposes of a private household. Apart from the limited situations specifically allowed by the legislation, however, no discrimination is lawful, regardless of the reasons for it. In tribunal proceedings, it is for the person complaining of discrimination to prove it.

However, unless a case seems hopeless the tribunal will want to hear what an employer has to say. Workers can put questions to the employer on a standard form before commencing a case. The answers given can be used in evidence and the tribunal can draw its own conclusions if the employer fails to reply.

Unlawful indirect discrimination occurs when an employer lays down requirements for a job which appear not to be discriminatory but where in practice it is considerably harder for persons of a particular sex or race to comply with them. Requiring job-holders to wear a uniform which is incompatible with their ethnic traditions comes into this category (such as forbidding the wearing of turbans or beards). Requiring a specified period of prior residence or work experience in the United Kingdom, or accepting only British qualifications, would also be covered. In one case an upper age limit of twenty eight on a job was held to discriminate against women, who are often out of the job market below that age. Requiring a substantial overtime or mobility commitment may also discriminate against women, who tend to have greater domestic responsibilities. Requiring a job to be performed full, rather than part, time may be discriminatory, depending on the circumstances. Employers can defend requirements which have a discriminatory effect by arguing that they are needed for the job. In one case a chocolate manufacturer defended a 'no beards' rule on grounds of hygiene. Demanding a particular level of educational attainment or literacy may also be justified by the nature of the job, although this level should not be pitched unduly high. In every case employers should examine their job requirements to see whether they could be discriminatory. If so, they should assess whether they are really necessary or whether the same result could be achieved in a non-discriminatory way. As in the case of direct discrimination, intention to discriminate is irrelevant to the lawfulness of the action. However, no financial compensation can be awarded against employers who satisfy the tribunal that they had no intention of discriminating indirectly.

The anti-discrimination legislation requires employers to consider their recruitment practices from the earliest stage. Advertising a job in a publication which is unlikely to be read by persons of a particular sex or race could be a breach. So could confining applications to particular agencies, schools or residential areas which do not themselves contain a racially or sexually balanced mix. Employers should look at the contents of advertisements to check that they do not conceal a discriminatory message. The use of job descriptions with sexual connotations, such as 'waiter' or 'salesgirl', show an intention to discriminate unless the contrary is clearly shown. When conducting interviews, employers should ensure that questions relate only to the requirements of the job. Questions about domestic commitments or family intentions should be avoided. Employers are liable for discriminatory actions by their workers unless they can show that they took all reasonably practicable steps to prevent them. Having and applying a clear equal opportunities policy would almost certainly provide a defence in this respect.

The legislation does not require employers to discriminate in favour of disadvantaged groups; indeed, doing this would be unlawful. There is a limited exception in relation to discriminatory training for jobs where during the preceding twelve months there were no, or comparatively few, members of a particular sex or race doing them. That apart, however, there is nothing to stop employers having 'positive action' programmes designed to encourage members of disadvantaged groups from applying for jobs or promotions.

Under the Sex Discrimination Act 1986, it is unlawful

to discriminate between men and women on grounds of age in relation to promotion, training and other employment opportunities. It is also unlawful to dismiss a woman because of her age when a man of that age would not be dismissed. Other provisions relating to death or retirement, such as when pensions become payable, are excluded from the legislation.

Trade Unionists and Non-Trade Unionists

It is unlawful for employers to discriminate against employees on grounds of their trade union membership once they are in employment. It is also unlawful to discriminate against non-trade unionists unless there is a valid closed shop agreement in force. These provisions are discussed in greater detail in Chapter 21.

Disabled persons

The Disabled Persons (Employment) Act 1944 requires employers of twenty or more persons to give employment to a quota, currently three per cent., of registered disabled persons. Certain employments are excluded. It is a criminal offence not to do this but only the Secretary of State for Employment may authorise prosecutions. In practice these provisions are not enforced.

Persons with a criminal record

The Rehabilitation of Offenders Act 1974 provides that after a certain period a conviction for a criminal offence becomes 'spent'. This period varies according to the gravity of the sentence. A non-custodial sentence becomes 'spent' after five years; a thirty-day prison sentence after seven. Imprisonment for a term exceeding thirty months can never be spent. Once a conviction becomes spent, the convicted person has no obligation to disclose it. It is unlawful to exclude a rehabilitated offender from any occupation or employment because they have a spent conviction or failed to disclose one. (Some occupations, such as doctors, accountants, teachers and health care workers, are excluded.) It is also unlawful to dismiss a person for that reason. There is no remedy under the 1974 Act for a person who is unlawfully excluded or dismissed. However, a dismissal based upon a spent conviction would be unfair under the Employment Protection (Consolidation) Act (see Chapter 19).

16 The Contract of Employment

The most basic rights and duties which employers and workers have depend upon the terms of the contract they negotiate. Rates of pay, hours of work, overtime, holidays, and the scope of a worker's job are all a matter for the parties to agree between them. There are some specific exceptions to this. In industries and services covered by wages councils orders, workers over twenty one can claim a minimum wage and employers who pay a lower rate can be prosecuted and fined. These sectors include retailing, catering, hairdressing and clothing manufacture. The law also restricts the hours which persons under eighteen may work in factories, hotels, laundries, and other specified areas. More generally, the law gives all employees statutory rights to certain payments, to minimum notice periods and to time off from work in particular situations. It also provides that men and women should receive equal pay for similar work or work of equal value. These provisions are discussed in Chapter 18. However, the fundamentals of the employment relationship are in most cases governed by the terms of the employment contract. In this chapter we shall begin by looking at the sources of contractual terms and the employer's obligation to issue a written statement which sets out the most important ones. We shall then look at the nature of the terms which the courts imply into contracts of employment unless the parties have agreed to the contrary. Finally, we shall consider the legal implications of changing employment terms and the remedies which are available if one of the parties breaks the contract.

Sources of Contractual Terms

The terms of an employment contract may be express or implied. Express terms are those which the parties have spelt out explicitly. Implied terms are those which the courts insert into a contract to make it work when the parties have left a matter open. The courts may insert such terms for one of three reasons. The first is to give effect to what they assume the intention of the parties must have been. This may be done to make the contract work in a businesslike way or because it seems an obvious term to include. If, for example, the employee is a travelling salesman but his contract says nothing about the distances he can be expected to travel, the courts will imply a term into his contract which demarcates the scope of his mobility. (The considerations applicable to mobility are dealt with later in this chapter.) The second basis for inserting a term is if it is the custom and practice in a particular trade or industry to include it. For this to happen, the term must be reasonable, certain and well known. The terms of collective agreements, discussed below, may be implied into contracts on this ground. Lastly, there are certain terms which the courts see as necessary to all employment relationships. These include the mutual obligations of co-operation and the employee's duty of faithful service.

Express terms of the contract may be determined by discussion between employer and employee as individuals. At the very least, the date an employee starts work will be settled by individual agreement and other terms, such as pay, hours or holidays, may also be arrived at by one-to-one negotiation. Alternatively, some or all of the terms of employment may be derived from a collective agreement. Collective agreements are agreements between an employer or employers' association and a trade union or unions which set out the terms on which particular groups of workers will be employed. Individual employers may themselves bargain with a union to reach such an agreement. Alternatively, they may simply decide to employ their workers on the basis of a national agreement covering their trade or industry. The majority of British workers are employed according to collective agreements, which apply regardless of whether the worker is a union member. Following such agreements has the advantage for employers of knowing that they are paying the 'going rate' for a job.

Collective agreements are not legally enforceable between employers and unions (unless the parties expressly decide that they should be). However, the terms of these agreements may be incorporated into individual contracts of employment. If this happens they can be enforced by either party like any other contractual terms. Incorporation may happen by express agreement or by implication. Express incorporation occurs when the parties expressly agree that their contract is subject to a particular collective agreement. Where the contract itself is not in writing, proof that the agreement has been incorporated may be helped if the written statement of employment terms, discussed below, makes reference to it. Implied incorporation can be based on custom and practice or business efficacy. Where it has been the practice in an industry or enterprise to follow a particular set of collective agreements, the courts will be very ready to find that this has become a contractual obligation. Similarly, where an individual's contract is silent on a matter, such as the length of time for which sick pay will be paid, the courts may look to the relevant collective agreement to settle the issue.

Employers may sometimes wish to give their workers 'Works Rules' or some other document which sets out rules of conduct in the workplace. This may, for example, stipulate clothing requirements or disciplinary offences or describe how jobs should be performed. Such rules may become terms of workers' contracts if workers expressly acknowledge them as such. Alternatively, they may be seen as implied contractual terms on the grounds spelt out above.

The Written Statement of Employment Terms

There is no legal obligation to put an employment contract into writing. However, section 1 of the Employment Protection (Consolidation) Act 1978 requires employers to give employees a written statement setting out their basic employment terms. This must be done within thirteen weeks of the employment starting. The statement must state the terms of employment at a specified date not more than one week before it is given. The statement must identify the parties to the contract and specify the date when the employment began. It should also state when the employee's period of 'continuous employment' began, a concept explained in the following chapter. (Periods of employment with a previous employer may in circumstances therein explained count in this context.) The statement should also set out the following:

1 The scale or rate of the employee's remuneration or the method of calculating it
2 How often payment is made
3 Hours of work
4 Any terms and conditions relating to holidays and

holiday pay; sickness and injury and sick pay; and
pensions and pension schemes
5 The length of notice each party must give to end the
contract. (For minimum periods laid down by law,
see Chapter 18)
6 The employee's job title.

If there are no terms on any of these matters, the statement should say this.
· The purpose of this provision is to give employees
information. The Act also allows the statement to refer
the employee to a collective agreement or some other
document for details of these matters instead of setting
them out in full. The employee must have resonable
access to such a document. As previously stated, reference to such a document may facilitate proof that it has
been incorporated into the employee's contract.
As well as these specified matters, the 1978 Act also
requires the written statement to include a note which

1 States whether the employer has an occupational
.pension scheme which has a certificate that it is
'contracted-out' of the state pension scheme under
the Social Security Pensions Act 1975
2 Specifies any disciplinary rules which apply to the
employee or refers him to some reasonably accessible
document which specifies them
3 Specifies a person to whom the employee can apply
if he is dissatisfied with any disciplinary decision
relating to him
4 Specifies a person to whom the employee can apply
if he has a grievance relating to his employment and
the manner of making such an application
5 Where there are further steps consequent upon an
application under (3) or (4) explains those steps or
refers the employee to a reasonably accessible document which explains them.

These last four obligations do not apply to decisions, grievances or procedures relating to health and safety at work. As Chapter 20 explains, these must be covered in a statement of general policy regarding health and safety matters.

Employers are not obliged to issue a written statement to employees who normally work for less than sixteen hours a week unless they have worked for eight hours or more for five years. However, employers may still wish to give part-timers statements to clarify their position. The obligation is also inapplicable where employees have a written contract covering all the matters specified.

The written statement is not a written contract. It merely sets out terms which have already been agreed. In cases of dispute, however, it provides strong, but not conclusive, evidence of the nature of the terms it covers. Where these terms change, the employee must be given a statement to this effect within one month. Any such change must have been agreed between the parties in accordance with the principles discussed below. Merely giving the employee a revised statement does not itself effect a valid change. Where the employer has referred the employees to another document for details of the terms, there is no need to inform him of individual changes provided that the original statement indicated that any changes would be entered in that document.

If an employer fails to provide him with a written statement, or it is incomplete, the employee can complain to an industrial tribunal. In addition, either party can go to a tribunal if the statement's accuracy is in doubt. The tribunal may determine the details of any particulars which are missing or amend those which it finds to be incorrect.

The Terms Which Courts Will Imply

As already stated, the courts may insert terms into contracts to fill in 'gaps' where there is no express provision but the relationship requires some term to exist. In doing this, the courts will look at all the circumstances, including the parties' practices since the contract was made. One area in particular where this has happened is in defining an employee's place of work. The contract may, and desirably should, make clear the extent to which an employee is required to be mobile in his job. If it does not, and an employer seeks to move an employee against his will, a term defining mobility will have to be implied. Its nature will depend upon several factors, including the nature of the business, whether there is any provision for overnight expenses and previous practice. In one case a mining tunneller was required to move to a different site. He did not want to do this. The court said that as the employers were contractors who worked at different sites, some mobility must have been envisaged, and the employee had in fact moved to different places in the past. The court concluded that he could be told to work anywhere within daily travelling distance of his home. In the case of more static employment, such as working in an office, the extent of mobility implied may be much narrower. Even so, there will probably be a little. When an office worker was required to transfer from Holborn to Regent Street in London the court decided that her place of work was Central London and not just the Holborn premises.

The courts have followed a similar line in relation to occupational sick pay. At one time it was assumed that if the contract said nothing, sick pay should be paid. In 1982, however, the Court of Appeal decided that this should be the case only if investigation of the circumstances failed to provide any clues. In this case, the employee had never been paid it in the past, nor had his fellow workers, and the court decided that he had no claim. In another case where it had previously been paid but the length of entitlement was uncertain, the court looked at the industry's collective agreement to settle the issue. Clearly if employers comply with their obligation to give details of sick pay in an employee's written statement, disputes of this nature should not arise.

As well as this 'gap-filling' kind, the courts imply certain terms into employees' contracts as a matter of law unless the contract states otherwise. If the employer breaches one of these terms and the employee resigns, this may mean he has been 'constructively dismissed', a concept discussed in Chapter 19. If the employee commits a serious breach, immediate dismissal may be justified. Again, this is discussed further in Chapter 19. In brief, the most basic implied terms are as follows:

1 *The duty of mutual co-operation.* On the employee's side, this requires obedience to the employer's lawful and reasonable orders as to how to perform the job. On the employer's, it requires that the relationship of trust and confidence is not undermined. This extends to preserving appropriate psychological as well as material conditions. So, for example, the term may be breached if an employer fails to investigate legitimate grievances, subjects an employee to gratuitous insults or upbraids an employee in front of subordinates. It does not generally require that employees are provided with work provided that the employer continues to pay them. (For the law on lay-offs, see Chapter 18). There are certain exceptions, however. In the case of pieceworkers or workers paid by commission, the employer must provide a reasonable amount of work. Contracts where the employment carries the opportunity of becoming better known, such as for actors or artists, are also

exceptions. Lastly, for skilled workers there may be a duty to provide sufficient work to maintain or develop existing skills.

2 *The employee's duty of faithful service*. Employees must serve their employers faithfully and honestly. They must not misappropriate the employer's property or make any secret profit from the job. Nor may they disclose the employer's trade secrets to third parties or misuse confidential information acquired in the course of their employment. 'Trade secrets' may cover matters such as secret processes of manufacture, for example chemical formulae, designs or special methods of construction. Confidential information may include matters such as customer lists. The obligation not to disclose 'trade secret's may continue even after the employment has ended. An employer who wishes to ensure the permanent protection of specific information, however, should insert an express term to that effect in the contract. If an employee threatens to disclose confidential information the employer may seek an injunction to prevent this.

There is no general implied limitation on employees undertaking spare-time work provided they do not damage their employer's business by, for example, working for a competitor. An employer who wishes to restrict spare-time working, or to make it subject to his or her permission, must make this a term of the contract.

3 *The duty of reasonable care*. Employers must take reasonable care for the safety of employees in the course of their employment. The Unfair Contract Terms Act 1977 prevents an employer from limiting this duty: any contractual term which restricts liability for death or personal injury resulting from negligence is void. For employees' part, they must exercise reasonable care and

skill in the performance of their duties. Technically, employees are liable to indemnify their employer against any damages the employer has to pay to third parties as a result of their negligence. (The employer's liability is based on vicarious liability as explained in Chapter 15). In practice, however, this rarely arises because employers are generally insured against most forms of liability. Since 1972 it has been compulsory for employers to take out insurance against injury to their employees.

Varying the Contract

The terms of an employment contract may change over time. At the very least, employees' wages will periodically increase. Employers may also sometimes want to alter working conditions or practices, hours or duties in ways to which employees object. What is then the position? Where such a change is contained in a collective agreement, the employees' terms will change automatically provided that their contracts incorporate it. Where, however, the contract does not allow for a particular change to be made, it will have to be varied. This requires the consent of both parties. Consent may be given expressly. It may also be implied from conduct if an employee works on the new terms. Sometimes, however, an employee may face the choice of accepting an adverse change or unemployment. In this situation, the courts will allow the employee a period of time, perhaps some weeks, to make up his mind. The period of time may be longer if the employee makes clear to the employer his dissatisfaction. If the employee ultimately resigns from the job, this may mean he or she can claim to have been constructively dismissed. However, as Chapter 19 makes clear, this does not automatically mean that the dismissal is unfair.

An employer who wishes to impose a contractual change may also choose to terminate employees' contracts with appropriate notice and offer re-engagement on the new terms. If employees refuse to accept this offer, they will have been dismissed and may again be able to claim for unfair dismissal.

Whether a change in working conditions requires the contract to be varied may not always be clear. New technology presents particular problems in this regard. If an employee is told to do the same job by different methods, does this involve a contractual change? The broad answer appears to be 'no'. In one case, tax officers were told to change from manual to computerised record-keeping. They claimed that the employers were not entitled to order this. The court turned down their case on the basis that their job function remained the same and the employers were entitled to change the method of performing it. The court added the rider, however, that had the employer required the employee to acquire 'esoteric' skills, its decision might have been different. The legal implications of new technology are discussed further in Chapter 19.

Remedies if the Employment Contract is Breached

If one party breaches the employment contract, the other may sue for damages. Employees may also sue for arrears of pay. Damages are calculated to compensate the injured party for losses which would ordinarily arise from such a breach together with any losses which were reasonably forseeable by the parties as likely to result. As Chapter 14 explains, claims for damages must be brought in the ordinary civil courts.

If the breach is sufficiently serious, it entitles the injured party to treat the contract as ended. Where the employee commits such a breach, for example by stealing from the employer, it entitles the employer to dismiss without notice. Where the employer commits such a breach, an employee who resigns has been 'constructively dismissed' (on which see Chapter 19).

Where a breach of contract is threatened or continuing, the injured party may seek an injunction to restrain it. An employer may wish to seek such a remedy if an employee is threatening to disclose confidential information about the business.

17 Continuity of Employment

To qualify for many of the statutory employment rights described in this book, employees need a minimum period of 'continuous employment'. For example, to claim a statutory guarantee payment, discussed in Chapter 18, an employee must have four weeks' continuous employment. Claims for unfair dismissal normally require two years' continuous employment. To count for continuity purposes, the requisite period of employment must be with the employer against whom the employee is claiming. (There are certain exceptional situations, outlined below, where employment with a previous employer also counts.) This employment may be under a single contract. Alternatively, it may be under a series of contracts, perhaps involving a number of different jobs. Employment is presumed to be continuous unless the contrary is shown. The rules for determining periods of continuous employment are set out in Schedule 13 of the Employment Protection (Consolidation) Act 1978. This chapter outlines the major principles.

Weeks which count

Periods of continuous employment are calculated in terms of 'weeks which count' for this purpose. For a week (which ends on a Saturday) to count, it must be either:

1 A week in which the employee has actually been employed for sixteen hours or more, or

2 A week for all or part of which the employment relationship is governed by a contract which normally involves employment for sixteen hours or more. This means that weeks during which an employee is absent because, for example, of illness or holidays, still count.

The requirement that the employee must work or normally work sixteen hours or more a week excludes part-time workers from many employment rights. However, if an employee works under a contract normally involving eight hours or more work a week, after five years he or she is treated like a full-time employee. The five years' service then count for continuity purposes and the employee can qualify for all the statutory rights.

If an employee who has worked under a contract involving employment for at least sixteen hours a week has his or her contractual hours reduced to eight or more, the weeks worked under the new arrangement continue to count for up to twenty six weeks.

Breaks in continuity

In general, if a week occurs which does not count for continuity purposes, continuity is broken. This means that the weeks already credited are wiped out and the employee has to start again. So if, for example, an employee works for sixteen hours for six weeks, then for six hours for six weeks, then again for sixteen hours a week, the first six weeks employment will not count. There are two situations, however, where weeks do not count but where continuity is still preserved. These are when an employee is either on strike or is locked-out by the employer. Weeks during which this happens do not count however short the strike or lock-out.

Weeks During Which There is no Contract of Employment Which Still Count

In general, if the employment relationship ends continuity will be broken. This is so even if the employee later returns to the same employer. However, there are four situations in which there may be no contract in existence for a period of time but which still count as periods of employment for continuity purposes if the employee returns to the job. Because these periods count, continuity is preserved. These situations are weeks during all or part of which:

1 The employee is incapable of work due to sickness or injury (assuming that the contract has been terminated). This applies up to a maximum of twenty six weeks;

2 The employee is absent due to a 'temporary cessation of work'. This covers the situation where the employee temporarily stops working as well as where the employer's business temporarily closes down. To determine if a cessation is indeed 'temporary' requires looking at the length of the gap in employment in relation to the whole period of employment. In one case, a teacher worked for eight years under a series of contracts, each lasting from September until the following July. It was held that the summer holidays, during which she had no contract, amounted to a 'temporary cessation'. She therefore had eight years' continuous employment;

3 The employee is absent in circumstances where by arrangement or custom he is regarded as continuing in employment. This would apply, for example, if it were the custom in the industry that an employee who left the employment and later returned were treated as having been employed throughout for pension or seniority purposes;

4 The employee is absent because of pregnancy or confinement. This applies up to a maximum of twenty six weeks. If an employee exercises her statutory right to return to work after pregnancy, described in Chapter 18, all the weeks she is absent count for continuity purposes.

Change of Employer

Normally continuous employment is built up only in employment with the same employer. There are four situations, however, where a period of continuous employment with one employer is carried over into employment with the next. These are:

1 Where the undertaking in which the employee works is transferred as a going concern from one employer to another. The precise meaning of 'transfer of an undertaking' is discussed in Chapter 19.

2 Where the employee is taken into the business of an 'associated employer'. Employers are 'associated' if one is a company of which the other employer has control or if both are companies of which a third person has control. 'Control' means control by the majority of votes attaching to shares exercised in general meeting.

3 Where the employee is employed by the personal representatives or trustees of a deceased employer.

4 Where there is a change in the partners in a partnership.

18 Legislation and Conditions of Employment

As Chapter 16 stated, in most industries the major terms of employment are regulated by contract. There are, however, three main areas where legislation gives employees (and, in some cases, all workers) some basic rights. These are pay, notice periods and time off from work.

As regards pay, employers are required to issue employees with an itemised pay statement. There are also restrictions on making deductions from workers' pay. Employees can claim a minimum payment if they are laid off. They also claim Statutory Sick Pay and Statutory Maternity Pay in appropriate circumstances. Lastly, the law requires employers to pay equal pay to men and women provided that certain conditions are met.

Employment relationships can usually be ended by one or other party giving notice. The law provides for minimum periods to be given.

Unlike many countries, British law says little about hours of work and holidays. There are, however, several situations where employees are entitled to time off during working hours. In addition, women are allowed a minimum period of maternity leave.

In this chapter we describe these basic rights.

Pay

Itemised pay statements

Section 8 of the Employment Protection (Consolidation) Act 1978 gives all employees the right to a written pay statement each time they are paid. This statement must itemise:

- the gross amount of wages or salary (excluding any customers' tips)
- variable and fixed deductions
- the net amount of wages or salary payable
- where different parts of the net amount are paid in different ways, the amount and method of each part-payment.

The employee need only be given the total amount of fixed deductions provided that he has previously received a written statement which gives details of each individual deduction. An employee can complain to an industrial tribunal if an employer fails to provide a statement. The tribunal can order the employer to pay the employee a sum not exceeding the unnotified deductions made in the thirteen weeks before the complaint was made. The right to an itemised pay statement applies only to employees who normally work sixteen hours or more a week (or who have worked at least eight hours a week for five years).

Deductions from wages

Under the Wages Act 1986, employers who make deductions from workers' pay must comply with certain requirements. (These also apply where employers require workers to make payments to them.) First, they must ensure that they have legal authority to make the deduction. This may be given by the workers' contract (by either an express or an implied term). Deductions for misconduct, carelessness, or other disciplinary reasons will require such a term. Alternatively, authority may arise from general legal principles. (For example, employers have a right to recover at least small overpayments of wages on this basis). Lastly, deductions may be authorised by statute. Employees' tax and national insurance payments come into this category.

Except where authority comes from statute, employers must then follow a special notification procedure. If the deduction is authorised by the statute, written notification of the authorising term must be given to the employee before any deduction is made. Alternatively, employers must obtain the worker's written agreement to the deduction, again before it is made. If the contract is varied to permit deductions in new situations, this new term can only cover conduct occurring after the variation takes effect. The Act covers deductions from any sum payable by the employer in respect of the worker's employment. It thus covers holiday pay, bonuses etc., and not just basic pay.

Certain types of deduction are excluded from the Act. (They still, of course, require there to be some legal authority to make them.) These include deductions made:

- to reimburse the employer for an overpayment of wages or expenses
- where there is a statutory requirement to make payments to a statutory authority (tax and national insurance, for example)
- where there is a 'check-off' arrangement with a trade union and the worker has agreed to the deduction
- where the worker has taken part in a strike or other

industrial action. (See Chapter 22 for the legality of doing this)

- where there is a court order requiring the worker to pay a sum to the employer, if the worker has agreed to this.

Underpayments due to an error in computing the worker's gross wage are also excluded.

The legislation covers both employees and those working under contracts personally to perform any work or service. (Situations where the employer is in reality a client or customer of the worker are excluded.) Where a deduction (or payment) which requires notification is made without it, or without proper authority, the worker can complain to an industrial tribunal. The tribunal can then order the employer to repay the amount unlawfully deducted or received. The employer cannot reclaim this money by a later deduction or demand.

Special provisions apply to workers in 'retail employment'. In the case of these groups, where the deduction is made because of a cash shortage or stock deficiency, the total amount deducted on a particular pay day may not exceed ten per cent of the worker's gross wage. (The same limitation applies to payments to the employer.) 'Retail employment' goes well beyond shops. It covers any employment involving, regularly or irregularly, 'retail transactions' directly with the public, fellow workers, or other individuals in their personal capacities. It also covers the collection of amounts payable in connection with retail transactions carried out by other persons. A 'retail transaction' means the sale or supply of goods or the supply of services (including financial services).

If the amount the employer is owed exceeds ten per cent of the worker's gross wage, the balance may be recovered on subsequent pay days. The ten per cent limit must always be observed, however, except in relation to the workers' 'final instalment of wages'. Then the employer can deduct any amount allowed by the contract. The 'final instalment' covers wages which consist of or include contractual remuneration in respect of the last of the periods for which the worker was employed under his contract. It also includes any payments in lieu of notice made after the contractual remuneration was paid.

Where it applies, the ten per cent limit covers situations where the deduction is attributed to conduct producing the shortage or deficiency, such as carelessness, as well as where it is attributed to the shortage itself. Deductions for these reasons must be made within twelve months of the employer discovering the shortage or deficiency (or within twelve months of the time he ought reasonably to have discovered them). If the penalty is in the form of a demand for payment, rather than a deduction, the employer must notify the worker in advance of his total liability and make a written demand for payment on one of the worker's pay days.

If the employer makes a deduction or receives a payment which exceeds the ten per cent limit, again the worker can complain to an industrial tribunal. The tribunal can order payment of the excess.

Payment during lay-offs and short-time working

An employer may need to 'lay-off' his workforce, or reduce their working hours, for a temporary period. This may happen where, for example, there is a shortage of components or a shortfall in orders. If the employer continues to pay the workers at their normal rate, usually no legal problem arises. As Chapter 16 explained, generally there is no obligation to give an employee work, only to continue payment. If an employer wants to reduce payments, or cease them altogether, however, there must be a term in the contract which permits this. Some industries have 'guaranteed week agreements' allowing a certain reduction in pay.

There may be one narrow exception to the principle that an employer must continue payment unless the contract otherwise provides. In a 1926 decision, the court held that when a colliery was closed temporarily for safety reasons, there was no need to maintain payments. This was because the circumstances causing closure were beyond the employer's control and the court implied a term into the contract that such risks would be shared. In an earlier case, however, a lay-off due to a trade recession was deemed within the employer's control. It is likely that nowadays the courts would restrict the circumstances in which the obligation to pay is averted.

Even if an employee's contract permits the employer to lay-off without pay, section 12 of the Employment Protection (Consolidation) Act 1978 gives all employees certain minimum rights. Employees who have been continuously employed for four weeks or more can claim a 'guarantee payment' of up to £10.70 if they are laid-off for a whole day. This payment (whose upper limit is periodically raised) is set off against any payment made under the employee's contract and vice versa. It is payable for up to five workless days in any three-month period. If an employer fails to make a payment, the employee can complain to an industrial tribunal. An employee is not entitled to a guarantee payment if the lay-off is caused by industrial action involving his employer or an associated employer (defined in Chapter 17). Entitlement is also lost if the employee unreasonably refuses to do suitable alternative work for the workless day or fails to comply with the employer's reasonable requirements to keep himself available for work. Employees who are employed on fixed term contracts for three months or less cannot claim guarantee payments. (A fixed term contract is defined in Chapter 19).

Sick Pay

Most employees in this country are entitled to sick pay from their employers under their contracts. It is up to employers to decide whether to make such provision. Whether or not sick pay is payable and if so, at what rate, must be set out in the employee's written statement of employment terms, described in Chapter 16. Regardless of what the contract says, employers have a statutory obligation to pay statutory sick pay (SSP) to all employees who are liable to pay Class I National Insurance contributions. There are three different rates, depending on the employee's normal weekly earnings. Employers can reclaim SSP from National Insurance contributions. Details of when SSP is payable, which are somewhat complex, are available from the DHSS. Payments of SSP are set off against any contractual payments which the employer may make and vice versa.

Maternity Pay

Like SSP, employers are responsible for administering Statutory Maternity Pay (SMP). SMP, too, can be reclaimed from National Insurance contributions. SMP is payable to women who leave work between the eleventh and sixth weeks preceding the expected week of confinement. It is payable for eighteen weeks. To qualify for SMP, a woman must be liable for Class 1 National Insurance contributions. There are two rates of SMP depending upon the period of employment. A minimum of twenty-six weeks' employment by the fourteenth week before the expected week of confinement is required. As with sick pay, employers may assume liability for maternity pay under the employee's contract. Any contractual liability is set off against SMP and vice versa. Further details on SMP are available from the DHSS.

Equal Pay

The Equal Pay Act 1970 (as amended) requires employers to pay equal pay to men and women in three situations. First, if they are doing 'like work'. Second, if they are doing work which has been 'rated as equivalent' under a job evaluation study. And lastly, if they are doing work of 'equal value'. It also requires them to give men and women equal treatment in respect of all other terms and conditions covered by the contract. Matters such as sick pay and holidays are therefore included, for example. Special treatment given to women in connection with pregnancy or childbirth is explicitly excluded. This means that men cannot use the Act to claim paternity leave. Women should not be required to retire earlier than men but other provisions relating to death or retirement are excluded. The Act covers both employees and those who work under other contracts personally to execute any work or labour.

Equal treatment must be given to men and women who work 'in the same employment'. This means employment by the same employer or any 'associated employer' (see Chapter 17 for definition) at the same establishment or another establishment where common terms and conditions are observed.

Where one of the three tests above is satisfied, the contracts of men and women doing the work include an 'equality clause'. This modifies any term which is less favourable than that in the contract of a person of the opposite sex to make it no less favourable. Thus, for example, if a man and a woman are doing like work but the man is paid £200 a week and the woman £160, the woman's wage is put up to £200. A woman (or a man) who considers that an equality clause should be present in their contract can complain to an industrial tribunal. (Employers, too, can refer equal treatment issues.) Comparison must be made with an actual, rather than a hypothetical, person of the opposite sex. However, that person need not be in the employment simultaneously. Comparison can therefore be made with a predecessor in a job. If the tribunal upholds the complaint, it can award arrears of pay and damages going back for up to two years.

'Like work' means work 'of the same or a broadly similar nature'. A wide approach is taken to this. In one case, a woman cook who prepared some twenty lunches each day for a company's directors was held to be doing 'like work' with male canteen cooks who prepared 350 lunches a day over six sittings. Their work was of the same type and required similar skill and knowledge. However, differences of 'practical importance' between the two jobs may prevent there being 'like work' if these are the sort of differences one would expect to see reflected in different terms and conditions. If one worker has greater obligations than the other, this may be sufficient. Regard must be had to how often these obligations are performed in practice as well as what the contract says. Mere differences on paper are not enough. In one case, men working on the counter at a betting shop were paid more than the women. The employers argued that this was because they had to deal with trouble from customers. In practice, they never had to perform this role. The women were entitled to equal pay. The time at which work is done is not a difference of 'practical importance'. Employers can pay special premiums for night working, or other unsocial hours, but the basic pay of workers doing 'like work' must be the same.

Employers may decide to conduct a job evaluation study. Such a study evaluates all workers' jobs by giving them points under various headings such as effort and skill. If a man's and a woman's jobs are given equal ratings under the scheme but they are not afforded equal treatment, the disadvantaged party may complain.

The last ground for claiming equal pay is that the work of a comparator is of 'equal value'. Value is measured in terms of job content rather than, say, profitability. This test can be used only if neither of the first two applies. To help the tribunal decide if two jobs are indeed of 'equal value' an 'independent expert' from a panel appointed by ACAS prepares a report. The worker and employer can cross-examine the expert at the hearing and call one expert witness each of their own. The tribunal then makes its own decision. In one early case, a female cook successfully claimed her job was of equal value to those of painters and joiners in a shipyard.

If an employer has carried out his or her own job evaluation study, and two jobs have been given different ratings under it, no claim can be made that the jobs are of equal value unless the study itself discriminates on grounds of sex. This may happen if the study attributes disproportionate weight to skills connected with jobs performed by one sex or the other, such as physical strength. Provided that the study is conducted properly, however, it may help an employer to avoid being subject to equal value claims.

Employers have a defence to unequal treatment even though one of the three tests is satisfied. Where there is 'like work' or 'work rated as equivalent', the employer can claim that the discrepancy, is genuinely due to a 'material difference' other than that of sex.

This usually relates to the personal circumstances of the worker. A longer period of service, greater experience, age and higher qualifications are the most common 'material differences'. Market forces are not generally a defence here; employers cannot argue, for example, that they could only get a man by paying him a higher rate. Where, however, the comparator is a predecessor, an employer may be able to argue that the economic circumstances changed between the two employments and any successor, regardless of sex, would have been treated less well. Where the claim is based on 'equal value', the employer has greater scope to use market forces arguments, such as skill shortages. In equal value cases, the defence can be put forward before the independent expert prepares his or her report.

Both men and women can invoke the Equal Pay Act. In practice, however, women have suffered less favourable treatment more often than men. Employers should examine their pay structures carefully to ensure that they do not inadvertently discriminate on grounds of sex.

Rights to Notice

How long an employment relationship lasts depends on the parties' contract. Occasionally a contract is made for a fixed period such as three years. This sometimes happens in the case of senior management, technical specialists and teachers. In this situation, the relationship cannot be ended sooner unless one or other party commits such a serious breach of contract that the other has the option of treating the relationship as over. Most contracts, however, can be ended by one side or the other giving notice. The length of notice required should be spelt out in the contract. If not, it may be implied from custom. If the contract says nothing, the courts require a 'reasonable' period of notice to be given. What is 'reasonable' depends on the circumstances, including the employee's length of service, seniority, and how often he or she is paid.

Regardless of what the contract says, section 49 of the Employment Protection (Consolidation) Act 1978 lays down minimum notice periods for employees. These take effect if the contractual period is lower. If it is higher, then the contract prevails. Under the Act, an employer must give at least one week's notice to a person who has been 'continuously employed' (see Chapter 17) for four weeks or more but less than two years. If the employment is for two years or more, the minimum period is one week's notice for every year of service up to a maximum of twelve weeks' notice. Thus, an employee who has been continuously employed for seven years is entitled to seven weeks' notice; an employee employed for fourteen years to twelve weeks. A 'week' means seven clear days. The only restriction on employees is that if they have been continously employed for four weeks or more they must give one week's notice. This provision does not prevent either side from waiving the right to notice or accepting a payment in lieu.

Time off During Working Hours

There are six situations in which employees are entitled to be given a reasonable amount of time off work during working hours by their employer. 'Working hours' mean times when the employee is required under the contract to be actually working, so lunch hours, for example, are not 'working hours'. The first five rights are granted by the Employment Protection (Consolidation) Act 1978. The first three are given only to employees who work sixteen hours or more a week;

part-timers are excluded unless they have worked for eight hours or more for five years. The sixth is given by the health and safety legislation, discussed in Chapter 20.

1 Officials of independent trade unions recognised by the employer are entitled to paid time off for certain industrial relations duties and training. This right is discussed in more detail in Chapter 21.

2 Members of independent trade unions recognised by the employer are entitled to unpaid time off for union activities and to represent the union. This is also covered in more detail in Chapter 21.

3 All employees are entitled to unpaid time off for specified public duties, including acting as a justice of the peace, member of a tribunal, and member of a local authority or governing body of an educational establishment. The time off may be used only for attending meetings and for executive functions. In deciding what is 'reasonable' here, regard may be had to the amount of time off required to perform the particular duty, the effect of the employee's absence on the business and the amount of time off taken for (1) and (2) above.

4 Employees who have been continuously employed for two years or more who are given notice of dismissal for redundancy (defined in Chapter 19) are entitled to paid time off during the notice period to look for new employment or make arrangements for training for future employment. Employees who are unreasonably refused time off may claim compensation of up to two-fifths of a week's pay. (This is subject to a statutory maximum, currently £155).

5 Pregnant employees are entitled to paid time off for an appointment for ante-natal care received on medical advice. A certificate or appointment card

must be produced for a second or subsequent appointment.

6 Safety representatives appointed by a recognised independent trade union are entitled to such paid time off as is necessary to perform their statutory functions and for reasonable training. This is discussed in more detail in Chapter 20.

In all six cases, an employee can complain to an industrial tribunal if the employer fails to grant the time off on request. For union officials and members, those performing public duties and safety representatives, the tribunal can make a declaration and award compensation. In assessing compensation, the tribunal will have regard to the employer's default and any loss the employee has suffered. A union official and safety representative may also be awarded the remuneration due to them. A redundant employee and a pregnant woman may claim the amount due to them.

Maternity Leave

Employers may choose to give all female employees the right to maternity leave under their contracts. Regardless of what the contract says, the Employment Protection (Consolidation) Act 1978 gives women minimum rights to return to work after pregnancy or confinement. The woman can exercise her right to return at any time up to twenty nine weeks from the week in which the date of confinement falls. She is entitled to return to her old job on terms and conditions no less favourable than if she had not been absent.

To qualify for this right, women must be employees; have continued in employment until immediately before the beginning of the eleventh week before the expected week of confinement; and must, at the beginning of that eleventh week, have been continuously employed for two years or more. They must also follow complex notification procedures. In outline, a woman must tell her employer in writing that she will be absent due to pregnancy or confinement, the expected week of confinement, and that she intends to return to work. She must do this at least twenty one days before her absence begins or as soon as reasonably practicable thereafter. If the employer so requests, she must produce a certificate stating the expected week of confinement signed by the doctor or midwife. If the employer later sends her a written request asking her to confirm in writing that she intends to return, she must reply within fourteen days of receiving it or as soon as reasonably practicable thereafter. The request should explain the consequences of a failure to reply. This request must be sent no sooner than forty nine days after the expected week of confinement. Lastly, the employee must tell the employer in writing of the date she proposes to return at least twenty one days before that date. The employee can later postpone this date on medical grounds for up to four weeks, even if this means going beyond the twenty nine week period. The employers, too, can postpone the date of return for up to four weeks if they give reasons. As Chapter 17 explains, a woman who exercises her right to return is treated for continuity purposes as if she had been employed throughout the period of absence.

If an employer refuses to allow a woman to return, she can complain of unfair dismissal. She is treated as if she had been employed until her notified date of return and as if she had been dismissed on that date for the reason she was not allowed to return. There are, however, three situations where the right to return is modified:

1 Where the employer shows that it was not reasonably

practicable to offer the employee her old job back but she is offered suitable alternative work. If she unreasonably rejects this offer, she has no claim.

2 If the woman cannot have her old job back because of redundancy, it is unfair not to offer her a suitable alternative vacancy if one exists. (This may be with the employer or an associated employer (defined in Chapter 17.)) If the woman turns down an offer, she cannot claim a redundancy payment but can still complain of unfair dismissal. If no vacancy exists, she is entitled to a redundancy payment.

3 If the total number of employees employed by her employer and any associated employer immediately before her absence did not exceed five, the employer is not obliged to take the woman back if it is not reasonably practicable to give her back her old job to offer suitable alternative work.

19 Discipline and Dismissal

In this chapter we look at how the law affects employers' powers to discipline and dismiss their employees. We begin by emphasising the need for a proper disciplinary procedure. This is for everyone's benefit. It means that both sides will know their position and will help employers in any unfair dismissal proceedings which may result. We then discuss specific legal controls over dismissal: the need to give correct notice and the need to act fairly. Lastly, we look at the legal position if redundancies are required or the undertaking is transferred to another employer.

Disciplinary rules and procedures

Every employer should have disciplinary rules and establish procedures for deciding when the rules have been breached. In the case of small employers, these rules may not be extensive. They may only cover matters such as safety, consideration for fellow employees, drunkeness and persistent absenteeism. Nevertheless, employees should always be given a written copy of the rules. This should set out the acts which constitute disciplinary offences and the penalties they may attract. (As stated in Chapter 16, the law requires information about disciplinary penalties to be issued with the written statement of employment terms.) The rules should also be explained to employees orally. Where a disciplinary penalty affects an employee's contractual rights, the right to impose the penalty must be in the contract. Suspension from work without pay and deductions from pay are two examples. When making deductions from pay, employers must comply with the Wages Act 1986, discussed in Chapter 18.

A.C.A.S. has issued a Code of Practice on Disciplinary Practice and Procedures in Employment. (For the effect of such Codes, see Chapter 14.) The Code encourages employers to involve employees in formulating rules. If employees are dismissed pursuant to an agreed procedure, tribunals nearly always find the dismissal fair. The procedure should allow employees to know the charge against them and have the opportunity of replying to it. They should have the right to be accompanied by a trade union representative or fellow employee of their choice when doing so. Charges should be investigated carefully. If the worker is suspended pending investigation, this suspension should be with pay. Any penalties imposed should be explained. If the business is sufficiently large, there should be a right to appeal to a higher disciplinary body.

The Code states that employees should not be dismissed for a first disciplinary offence unless there is gross misconduct. The rules should state what conduct will merit immediate dismissal. Stealing and fighting might be two examples. Where an offence is less serious, the employee should be given a formal warning, either orally or in writing depending on its gravity. It should be made clear that this is the first stage of the disciplinary procedure. If there is further misconduct, this may merit a final written warning. This should state the consequences of any further breach of discipline. The relevance of complying with the Code in unfair dismissal complaints is explained in the section which follows.

Controls over Dismissal

Notice

The first control over employers' power to dismiss is the contract. Employers must ensure that they give the correct period of notice. The periods required are discussed in Chapter 18. Failure to give adequate notice is a breach of contract and the employee will be able to bring proceedings in the civil courts (see Chapter 14). Sometimes a contract is for a fixed term, say three years. In that case the contract cannot lawfully be terminated before that period ends.

As explained in Chapter 16, the usual remedy for breach of an employment contract is damages. The employee who is dismissed with inadequate notice is entitled to claim the wages he or she would have earned during the proper notice period. Any earnings from other employment during this time are deducted. (So, too, is any amount the employee should have earned had he or she tried to get another job.) Also deducted are the amount of income tax and social security contributions which would have been payable had the sum been earned as wages; unemployment or supplementary benefit; and any unfair dismissal compensation which may have been awarded as a result of the dismissal.

Where employees commit a very serious breach of contract, employers may dismiss without notice if they choose. What constitutes a sufficiently serious breach is hard to determine in the abstract. The disciplinary procedure should spell it out. Sometimes the last in a line of several acts of misconduct can justify dismissal without notice. Where employers have followed the recommended procedure discussed above, employees will have realised that their job was in jeopardy.

The need to act fairly

Under section 54 of the Employment Protection (Consolidation) Act 1978, employees have the right not to be unfairly dismissed by their employer. This means that the employer must dismiss for a 'fair' reason and act reasonably in treating it as a sufficient reason for dismissal. We look at the categories of employee who are excluded from claiming unfair dismissal, the meaning of 'dismissal', the 'fair' reasons, the 'reasonableness' test and the remedies.

Excluded classes. The main categories of employee who cannot complain of unfair dismissal are:

1 Those with less than two years' continous employment on the date the contract ends. If the employee is dismissed for trade union membership or activities, or the lack of trade union membership, however, no minimum period of employment is required (see Chapter 21)
2 Those who have reached the normal retiring age for the job where this is the same for men and women. The normal retiring age is the age at which employees must retire unless special provision is made. If there is no such normal retiring age, the cut-off point is sixty-five.
3 Those who ordinarily work outside Great Britain
4 Those employed under fixed term contracts for one year or more who have waived their right to claim. A fixed term contract is one for a fixed period where the date of expiry is known. It may contain a provision for termination by notice before the term expires and still be a fixed term contract. To be valid, the waiver must be in writing and be made before the term expires. It only prevents an employee claiming where the term expires without renewal. (See the

meaning of 'dismissal' below.) It does not apply where the contract is terminated before that date.

The meaning of 'dismissal'. For statutory purposes, there is a dismissal in the following three situations:

1 Where the employer terminates the contract, with or without notice. If the termination is without notice, the employee may have a claim for breach of contract (see above). To be dismissed, the employee must have been given a definite termination date. A mere warning of future dismissal is not sufficient. If an employee is given the choice of resigning or being dismissed, this counts as a dismissal. Sometimes employers and employees agree to part company. Unless this is a genuine agreement, with no element of coercion by the employer, this will still be a dismissal. Employees who are under notice may themselves give notice to leave earlier. In this situation, they still retain the right to complain of unfair dismissal.
2 Where the employee is employed under a fixed term contract and the term expires without being renewed
3 Where the employee terminates the contract, with or without notice, in circumstances where he or she is entitled to terminate it without notice because of the employer's conduct. This refers to 'constructive dismissal ', where the employee resigns because the employer has committed a very serious breach of contract, or has indicated an intention to do this. Failing to pay an employee's wages, changing hours, job duties or other working conditions without agreement, or reducing pay are examples of such breaches. Breaching implied terms can also be sufficient. Breach of the duty of co-operation, discussed in Chapter 16, in a way which makes it very difficult for the employee to continue working is the commonest

example here. This covers matters such as subjecting the employee to unwanted sexual advances or gratuitous insults. A succession of breaches, culminating in a 'last straw', can be sufficient cause. The law gives employees a period of time after the breach, perhaps some weeks, to decide whether to resign. The period may be longer if the employee makes clear to the employer his or her dissatisfaction with the change. Once this period expires, the employee will be taken to have accepted the change (see Chapter 16, 'Varying the contract'). At this point, he or she can no longer claim to have been constructively dismissed.

In an unfair dismissal claim, it is for employees to prove dismissal.

Fair reasons. There are five reasons which the statute says are 'fair' reasons for dismissing an employee. These are:

1 A reason relating to the capability or qualifications of the employee for performing work of the kind which he or she was employed by the employer to do. 'Capability' includes skill, aptitude, health, or any other physical or mental quality
2 The employee's conduct
3 Redundancy (defined below)
4 Where continued employment would involve the employer or employee or both infringing legislation. One example would be if a driver is disqualified from driving
5 'Some other substantial reason of a kind such as to justify the dismissal of an employee holding the position which the employee held'.

An employee's unreasonable refusal to agree to changes in contractual terms has been one important reason within this 'catch-all' category. This will be particularly relevant if the employer wants to reorganise employees' working conditions to improve the efficiency of the business. He or she may, for example, want to alter working hours to extend job duties. Employers should be prepared to show the tribunal that they have good business reasons for requiring the employee to agree to the change. Other reasons which have been held 'substantial' are situations where the employee knew the employment was temporary, and strong personality clashes. Under the Act, dismissal of a temporary replacement for a woman on maternity leave is treated as a substantial reason provided that the replacement employee knew of the situation.

In unfair dismissal proceedings, the employer must prove a fair reason for dismissal. It is the real reason which is relevant here. Employers cannot substitute a reason which was unknown to them at the time of dismissal. If, for example, an employee is dismissed for absenteeism but the employer later finds he has been stealing, theft cannot be given as the reason. However, matters coming to light after dismissal may mean that the employee's compensation, if any, is reduced.

Under the statute, employees with six months' continuous employment can request from their former employer a written statement which sets out the reason for the dismissal. This must be supplied within fourteen days. It is admissible in evidence in any subsequent proceedings. If the employer unreasonably refuses to supply a statement, or the particulars in it are inadequate or untrue, the employee can complain to an industrial tribunal. If the tribunal upholds the complaint, it must award the employee two weeks' pay (subject to a maximum of £155 per week.)

The 'reasonableness' test. As well as having a fair reason to dismiss an employee, employers must also act 'reasonably' in treating it as a sufficient reason to dismiss in the circumstances. The size and administrative resources of the undertaking are relevant here. The tribunals do not ask whether they would themselves have dismissed the employee. The correct question is whether it was reasonable for the employer to do this. Provided the decision lies within a 'band of reasonable responses' to the situation, that is enough.

To support a decision to dismiss, employers must have reasonable grounds for their view of the facts. They cannot dismiss on mere suspicion. In cases of dismissal for misconduct or lack of capability, this will require full investigation of the facts. Following a fair procedure is essential. If employers follow the terms of the ACAS Code of Practice, discussed above, they should be protected against any claim. If they fail to follow a fair procedure, there is a strong chance that the dismissal will be held unfair unless the employer can show (which is hard) that the same decision would have been reached even if he had followed it. As the Code makes clear, employees should not be dismissed for a first offence or without notice except in cases of grave misconduct. Disciplinary offences which will lead to immediate dismissal should be spelt out in the disciplinary rules. Even so, employers should always consider each employee individually. In one case an employee of twenty years' standing was dismissed instantly for fighting. The disciplinary rules said that this would happen. Nevertheless, the dismissal was held to be unfair. The employers had failed to take account of the employee's long period of blameless service.

Whether conduct outside the workplace justifies dismissal depends on its nature. Problems sometimes arise when an employee is convicted of a criminal offence. According to the A.C.A.S. Code, employers should see whether the offence makes the employee unsuitable for the job or unacceptable to other employees.

For dismissals based on ill-health, employers should investigate the nature of the employee's illness and how long it is expected to last. They should discuss the matter with the employee. How long an employer should wait depends partly on the urgency of the need to find a permanent replacement. The size of the business may be very relevant here.

Where employers wish to reorganise their business in a way which requires changes in employees' contractual terms, they should discuss the changes with employees and see if any objections can be met. If they do this, but are forced in the end to dismiss an employee who rejects the change, the dismissal will probably be fair provided the employer has a good business reason for the change.

Where employees are to be made redundant, employers should give them as much warning as possible to enable them to look for other jobs. If alternative jobs are available within the undertaking or that of an associated employer, employers should seek to place the employees in them. Employees should be selected for redundancy according to objective criteria. 'Last in, first out' is a common pattern. Matters such as attendance record, efficiency and experience may also be relevant. It is always unfair to select employees because of their trade union membership or activities or lack of union membership and dismissed employees can claim a higher rate of compensation (see Chapter 21). It is also unfair to select them in contravention of an agreed procedure or customary arrangement within the undertaking unless there is a special reason justifying this. Employers should also bear in mind the sex discrimination law in this context. As Chapter 15 makes clear, dismissing part-timers before full-timers may be indirect discrimination against women. Where employers recognise a trade union, the law requires them to consult the union about impending redundancies (see Chapter 21).

Automatically unfair dismissals. There are three situations where a dismissal is always unfair:

1 Unfair selection for redundancy (discussed above).
2 Where a woman is dismissed because of her pregnancy or any reason connected with it, such as illness or her need for time off. There is an exception where the employee is incapable of doing her job because of her pregnancy, or cannot continue to do it under statute, at the date of dismissal. The fairness of her dismissal will then be assessed in the usual way provided that the employer shows that he had no suitable alternative work for her to do or that any such work was offered to her. Employers may wish to consider suspension rather than dismissal in this situation, however. The relationship between maternity leave and unfair dismissal is discussed in Chapter 18.
3 Where an employee is dismissed for membership of an independent trade union or participation in its activities, or for lack of union membership unless there is a valid closed shop. This is discussed further in Chapter 21.

Remedies. There are three remedies for an unfairly dismissed employee:

1 Reinstatement. This requires the employer to treat the employee as if he or she had never been dismissed. Any arrears of pay or other benefits must be made up
2 Re-engagement. For this remedy, the employee is employed in a new job which is comparable to the

old or otherwise suitable. It may be with a successor or an associated employer.

In deciding whether to order reinstatement or re-engagement, the tribunal takes account of the employee's wishes, whether he or she caused or contributed to the dismissal, and whether it is practicable for the employer to comply with the order.

3 Compensation. This falls into two parts: the basic award and the compensatory award. The basic award is calculated according to the employee's age and length of service. He or she gets one and a half week's pay for each year of employment over the age of forty one; one week's pay for each year between twenty two and forty and half a week's pay for each year under twenty two. The award is reduced by one twelfth for each month the employee is over sixty four. The maximum amount of a week's pay is currently £155. A maximum of twenty years' service is taken into account. The award may be reduced where employees caused or contributed to the dismissal, their conduct prior to the dismissal warrants a reduction, or where they unreasonably refused an offer of reinstatement. Any redundancy payment paid, or other amount referable to the basic award, is also deducted. The compensatory award is such amount as the tribunal considers 'just and equitable in the circumstances' having regard to the employee's loss, up to a maximum of £8,000. It takes account of the employee's loss of earnings to the date of the hearing, estimated future loss of earnings, loss of benefits (such as a company car), loss of statutory employment protection rights which require a minimum period of employment, loss of pension rights and any expenses in looking for a new job. A reduction may be made if the employee caused or

contributed to the dismissal or failed to look for a new job.

If an employer fails to comply with a tribunal order to reinstate or re-engage an employee, the employee will get a basic and compensatory award and a special additional award of between thirteen and twenty six weeks' pay (or twenty six to fifty two weeks' pay if the dismissal was due to sex or race discrimination.)

Redundancy

Employees who are dismissed for 'redundancy' are entitled to a minimum redundancy payment from their employer. (Many employers give more generous payments.) The payment is calculated in the same way as the basic award for unfair dismissal except that service under the age of eighteen does not count. (The deductions which may be made from the basic award do not apply here.) Employers who, together with any associated employer, employ fewer than ten employees can reclaim thirty five per cent of the payment from a Redundancy Fund which is financed by National Insurance contributions. To claim a payment, employees require two years' continuous employment from the age of eighteen. Employees over sixty five cannot claim. Employees employed under fixed term contracts for two years or more cannot claim for non-renewal of their contracts if they have agreed in writing to waive this right.

To claim a redundancy payment, employees must have been dismissed. 'Dismissal' here has basically the same meaning as for unfair dismissal. This means that 'constructive dismissal' is included. Employers often call for volunteers for redundancy. Employees who volunteer have still been dismissed. Employees who are given notice may leave earlier if they give the employer written notice during the 'obligatory period'. This means the period of notice which the employer is obliged to give. If the employer still wants the employee to work out his or her notice, he can demand this in writing. If the employer warns the employee that refusing to do this will put his or her redundancy payment in jeopardy and the employee refuses, the tribunal will decide whether the employee should get a payment (or part of it).

The meaning of 'redundancy'

Employees are 'redundant' if their dismissal is wholly or partly because of either:

1 The fact that their employer has ceased or intends to cease to carry on business in the place where the employee was employed. 'Place' of employment means the place where the employees can be told to work under their contracts. (See Chapter 16);

2 The fact that the requirements of the business for employees to carry out work of a particular kind in the place where the employees were employed have ceased or diminished or are expected to do so. This is referring to diminished requirements for the actual work not for the individual employee. In one case, a publican decided to replace a middle-aged barmaid with a young girl to give the pub a more lively image. The dismissed barmaid was not redundant; there was still bar work to be done. If the nature of a job changes, tribunals have to decide whether it has become work of a different kind. This is a question of degree. Employees are expected to adapt to new methods and techniques. The fact a job is done by different methods does not make it a different job unless possibly the change is very extreme. Requiring

clerical workers to use basic computers would not mean their job had changed. Neither are employees redundant because the employer changes their working hours or other conditions. However, a change from night work to day work may be sufficiently radical to constitute a wholly different job. There is a presumption that a dismissal is due to redundancy unless the contrary is shown. This means that in borderline cases the employee is given the benefit of the doubt.

Employees lose their right to a redundancy payment if, before their contracts end, their employer offers to keep them on, either in their old jobs or in suitable alternative ones, and they unreasonably refuse this offer. The new contract must take effect within four weeks of the old one expiring. Alternative employment may be with an associated employer, or, if the undertaking is transferred (see below), with a transferee employer. In looking at suitability, the tribunals look at status as well as salary. Whether an employee's refusal is 'unreasonable' depends on all the facts, including domestic circumstances. Where the offer is of a different job, employees have the right to a four week trial period in the job without prejudicing their rights.

Transfer of Undertakings

Under the Transfer of Undertakings (Protection of Employment) Regulations 1981, employees are given certain rights if an undertaking, or part of it, is transferred from one employer to another. They apply only if the business is a 'commercial venture'. It must be transferred as a going concern so that it is the same business in different hands. It is not sufficient that the physical assets are transferred. (If that is all that happens, employees of the transferor employer will be redundant.)

Where a business is transferred, the contracts of employees, and all the transferor's rights and duties in connection with the contracts, are transferred to the transferee employer. This means, among other things, that the employee's continuity of employment with the old employer is preserved and carried over into the new employment. In addition, any collective agreements are transferred, as is any trade union recognition provided that the undertaking maintains a distinct identity under the new employer. (For union consultation rights on transfers, see Chapter 21.)

If employees are dismissed by either the transferor or transferee because of the transfer, their dismissals are deemed unfair. However, if the reason for dismissal is an 'economic technical or organisational reason entailing changes in the workforce' of either employer, this is a 'substantial reason' for dismissal. Fairness will then depend on reasonableness. Factors such as who was selected, whether there was consultation, and whether efforts were made to find dismissed employees alternative employment will be relevant here. An employee dismissed for such a reason can still claim a redundancy payment in this context.

If the transferee employer makes substantial changes in employees' terms or conditions of employment, they can resign and claim to have been constructively dismissed. Reduction of transferred employees' pay by transferee employers to fit in with their own original workforce has been held not to be a 'reason entailing changes in the workforce.'

20 Health and Safety at Work

In this chapter we look briefly at the major duties of employers in relation to the health and safety of their workforce. Before 1974, safety legislation was restricted to particular groups of workers in specific activities or premises. The 1974 Health and Safety at Work etc. Act 1974 provides a broad framework for extending safety legislation to all workers. It also protects the public at large against risks from the activities of those at work. Employers should still check, however, whether there are any particular requirements relating to their kind of business.

As well as employers, the Act imposes general duties on employees, the self-employed, controllers of non-domestic premises used as places of work, and designers, manufacturers, importers and suppliers of articles and substances for use at work. Here we look only at the position of employers and employees.

The General Duties

The duties of employers

Employers have a duty to ensure, so far as is 'reasonably practicable', the health, safety and welfare at work of all employees. Youth Training Scheme trainees are also owed this duty. The rider of reasonable practicability requires the risk to health and safety to be balanced against the cost and trouble of controlling and removing the risk. As well as the maintenance of safe premises and a safe system of work, the employer's duty also includes the provision of information, training and supervision. Employers of five or more employees must prepare a written statement of their health and safety policy and its administration and bring this to employees' attention. This statement should be revised whenever appropriate.

Employers also have a duty to conduct their undertakings so as to ensure as far as reasonably practicable that non-employees are not exposed to risks to their health and safety. This duty too can involve providing appropriate instruction and information. Providing such information to non-employees may also be necessary to ensure the health and safety of employees. Self-employed persons have a similar duty with respect to themselves and others.

The duties of employees

Employees must take reasonable care for the health and safety of themselves and others who may be affected by their acts or omissions. Employees must also co-operate with others to enable them to carry out their statutory duties.

Enforcement procedures

It is a criminal offence for any person or corporate body to contravene these general duties or other statutory provisions or regulations. (Where an offence is committed with the consent of, or is attributable to any neglect by, any officer of a corporate body, that officer can also be prosecuted.) Inspectors employed by local authorities and the Health and Safety Executive have wide-ranging powers to enter premises and to carry out investigations. If inspectors discover that the law is being broken, they may institute a prosecution in either the magistrates' or the Crown Court, depending on the seriousness of the offence. The Crown Court can impose an unlimited fine and, for certain offences, up to two years' imprisonment. In addition, or instead, they may serve either an 'improvement' or a 'prohibition' notice. An improvement notice can be served if inspectors consider that a person is breaking the law or has done so and is likely to do so again. It requires the person to remedy the situation within a specified period. Prohibition notices can be served if inspectors believe that activities are being, or are about to be, carried on which involve a risk of serious personal injury. They direct that those activities should not be carried on under the control of the person on whom they are served unless matters are remedied. They can be issued with immediate effect. The person on whom an improvement or prohibition notice is served can appeal to an industrial tribunal within twenty-one days of service. An improvement notice is suspended in the meantime but a prohibition notice continues unless the tribunal orders otherwise. The tribunal can cancel, affirm or modify the notice as it sees fit. Contravention of an improvement notice is punishable by an unlimited fine, of a prohibition notice by a fine and/or two years' imprisonment.

Employee Participation

The 1974 Act provides for employee participation in health and safety matters. The relevant provision is the Safety Representatives and Safety Committee Regulations 1977. These enable independent trade unions to appoint safety representatives from among the employees of an employer by whom they are recognised. (See Chapter 21 for the meaning of 'independent' and 'recognised'.) The number of representatives is up to the employer and union or unions. If possible the representatives should have been employed by the employer for at least two years or have had two years' experience in similar employment. Employers must consult safety representatives on arrangements for enabling co-operation with employees in developing health and safety measures and in checking their effectiveness. Safety representatives also have other specific functions, including investigating potential hazards and employees' complaints. They are entitled to inspect the whole or part of the workplace at least every three months after giving the employer reasonable notice in writing. (These inspections may be more frequent if, for example, there are substantial changes in working conditions or new information comes to light.) Representatives are entitled to have private discussions with employees. They are also entitled to take copies of relevant documents and be furnished with information they require to perform their functions. The Health and Safety Commission has issued a Code of Practice which amplifies this duty. Inspectors have a duty to inform safety representatives of the results of their inspections of the workplace.

Safety representatives are entitled to be given such paid time off during working hours as is necessary to perform their functions and to undergo reasonable training. The Code of Practice gives guidance on what is 'reasonable' here. The remedy if an employer refuses to allow time off is described in Chapter 18.

An employer must establish a safety committee if at least two safety representatives request this in writing. The employer must consult all the safety representatives and representatives of recognised unions. The Committee must be established within three months of the original request. Its composition is for the parties to decide, but the Health and Safety Commission recommends that management representatives should not be in the majority. The Committee can determine its own brief.

A breach of the 1977 Regulations may result in an improvement notice being issued and a maximum fine of £400 on prosecution.

21 Employers and Trade Unions

In this chapter we outline the rights which trade unions and trade union members have in their dealings with employers. These rights are given only to 'independent' trade unions. These are unions which are free from control or interference by employers. Some staff associations do not meet this requirement. If a trade union has a 'certificate of independence' issued by the Certification Officer, that proves that it is independent. Some rights are also restricted to trade unions which are 'recognised' by employers. A union is recognised if an employer is willing to bargain with it over matters such as terms and conditions of employment, discipline and negotiating machinery. There may be a specific recognition agreement. Alternatively, recognition may be implied from a clear course of conduct over time.

We begin by discussing the rights which the law gives individual union members. We then look at the right not to join a union and the implications of having a closed shop. Lastly, we examine the rights of consultation and other rights which the law gives an independent recognised union.

The Rights of Union Members

The right to join an independent trade union and participate in its activities

All employees have the right to belong to an independent trade union. If an employer dismisses an employee for joining any such union, the dismissal is automatically unfair. No qualifying period of employment, or minimum number of hours work per week, is required to complain of unfair dismissal for this reason. It is also unfair to dismiss an employee for taking part in the activities of an independent trade union at an appropriate time. Any activities a union expressly or impliedly authorises a member to pursue are covered. 'Appropriate time' means outside working hours or inside them with the employer's consent. 'Working hours' are times when employees are required to be working under their contracts. This means that no permission is needed to hold union meetings or discuss union matters during lunch hours or other breaks. Employees should be allowed to participate in union activities on the premises provided that they do not cause substantial inconvenience to the employer or other workers.

Employees who are dismissed for their union membership or activities are entitled to enhanced unfair dismissal compensation. Provided they seek reinstatement or re-engagement, they are entitled to a special award of between £11,000 and £22,000. This is in addition to a minimum basic award of £2,200 (before deductions) and a compensatory award. The special award can be even higher if reinstatement or re-engagement is ordered and the employer refuses to comply. Employees who allege they have been dismissed for these reasons can seek 'interim relief'. The tribunal grants it if it thinks the complaint is likely to succeed. It requires the employer to provide the benefits of employment pending the full hearing.

Employees are also protected against 'action short of dismissal' for union membership or activities. This covers matters such as refusing promotion or pay rises or otherwise discriminating against them. Again no minimum period of employment is required to complain. Tribunals can award employees such compensation as is 'just and equitable' having regard to the infringement of their right and consequent loss.

Rights to time off work

As Chapter 18 explained, members and officials of independent trade unions recognised by the employer have rights to a reasonable amount of time off during working hours. Officials are entitled to paid time off to carry out duties concerned with industrial relations between their employer and any associated employer and employees. This can cover the discussion of union strategy with other officials as well as actual negotiations, and is not limited to the extent of recognition. Officials are also entitled to time off for training in aspects of industrial relations relevant to their duties and approved by the TUC or their union. Trade union members are entitled to unpaid time off for taking part in union activities and for activities in which they are acting as representatives.

Employers should attempt to reach agreement with union representatives on the principles governing time off in their particular enterprise. There is an A.C.A.S. Code of Practice which gives guidance on what is a 'reasonable' amount of time off to grant and what are 'reasonable' conditions to impose on it. The remedies available if employers fail to grant time off are described in Chapter 18.

The Right Not to Join a Union and the Closed Shop

In general, it is unfair to dismiss employees for refusing to join a trade union (independent or non-independent) on the same basis that it is unfair to dismiss for joining. It is also unlawful to take action short of dismissal against employees for such a reason. The same enhanced levels of unfair dismissal compensation apply. In addition, if employers claim they were induced to take action against complainants by industrial action or the threat of it, the person calling the industrial action or threatening it can be joined as a party to the proceedings. This may be done by either the employer or the complainant. The person (or union) joined may then have to pay some or all of the compensation awarded to the complainant.

A 'closed shop' or 'union membership agreement' exists where it is compulsory for employees of a particular class to join a specified independent union or one of a number. It is up to employers to decide whether they enter such agreements. (A Code of Practice gives some guidance on this.) If a closed shop exists, it is then fair to dismiss employees who refuse to join a specified union. There are a number of situations in which dismissal for this reason remains unfair, however:

1 Where the agreement has not been approved in a ballot within the five years preceding the employee's dismissal. Agreements taking effect before 14 August 1980 require the approval of at least 80 per cent. of those entitled to vote or 85 per cent. of those voting. The same applies to second or subsequent ballots. Agreements taking effect after that date require the approval of at least 80 per cent. of those entitled to vote;

2 Where the employee 'genuinely objects on grounds of conscience or other deeply held personal conviction to being a member of any trade union whatsoever or of a particular trade union';

3 Where the employee has never been a member of a specified union since the agreement took effect;
4 Where the employee has not been a member of the union since the date of the ballot approving an agreement taking effect after 14 August 1980;
5 Where the employee has started proceedings under the Employment Act 1980 alleging that he or she was unreasonably expelled or excluded from a specified union;
6 Where the employee is subject to a written code of conduct which prevents him or her from taking industrial action.

The same principles also apply to action short of dismissal.

Rights of Independent Recognised Trade Unions

The right to disclosure of information

In conducting collective bargaining, employers will often want to give union negotiators information about the state of the business. In addition, the Employment Protection Act 1975 obliges employers to disclose to union representatives on request any information about the undertaking (or that of an associated employer) without which they would be materially impeded in conducting collective bargaining, and which it would be good industrial relations practice to disclose. An A.C.A.S. Code of Practice gives some guidance on the kind of matters which will probably be covered. There are certain exceptions to this obligation. In particular, employers need not disclose information they received in confidence and information whose disclosure would cause substantial injury to the employer's undertaking other than for its effect on collective bargaining.

If the employer fails to disclose requested information, the union can complain to a tripartite independent body, the Central Arbitration Committee (CAC). The CAC gives a ruling. If the employer still refuses to disclose the information, the CAC can ultimately make an award as to the terms and conditions of the employees concerned. This award takes effect in their contracts.

The right to consultation on redundancies

The Employment Protection Act 1975 requires employers to consult union representatives when they plan to make any employees redundant. (For the meaning of 'redundant', see Chapter 19). The employees need not be union members as long as the union is recognised for employees of their description. 'Consultation' means telling union representatives in writing the reasons for the proposals, the numbers involved, the total numbers in that work category, the proposed method of selection and the proposed method of implementing the dismissals. Employers must consider union representatives' replies and give reasons if they reject their suggestions. Consultation must be 'at the earliest opportunity'. If employers propose to dismiss 100 or more employees at one establishment over a ninety-day period, they must consult at least ninety days before the first dismissal. If ten or more will be dismissed over thirty days, they must consult at least thirty days before. Where 'special circumstances' make it not reasonably practicable to comply with these time limits, consultation must be as soon as possible. These circumstances must be out of the ordinary. Insolvency which the employer saw, or should have seen, coming is not enough.

If employers fail to consult, the union can complain

to an industrial tribunal. The tribunal may make a 'protective award'. This keeps the employees on the payroll. The length of the award is up to the tribunal, subject to a maximum of ninety days where 100 or more employees are involved; twenty eight where there are fewer than ten. Any contractual remuneration is set off against this. If the employer fails to pay the award, employees can complain to the tribunal.

Employers are also required to notify the Department of Employment of any impending redundancies involving ten or more employees within the same time limits as the duty to consult. The penalty for not doing this is a £400 fine or loss of up to ten per cent of any redundancy rebate to which the employer would be entitled. There is a similar 'special circumstances' defence.

The right to consultation on transfer of the undertaking

The Transfer of Undertakings (Protection of Employment) Regulations are discussed in Chapter 19. They require both transferor and transferee employers to give information about the transfer to representatives of unions recognised for employees who may be affected by the transfer or measures taken in connection with it. Where either employer envisages that he or she will be 'taking measures' in relation to such employees, the appropriate union must be consulted. Again there is a 'special circumstances' defence. If an employer fails to consult or provide information, the union can complain to an industrial tribunal which can award up to two weeks' pay for each employee affected.

Rights in relation to health and safety

These are discussed in Chapter 20.

22   Industrial Action

In this chapter, we look at the legal situation when employees take industrial action. We look mainly at the consequences for the relationship between employers and individual employees. Employers faced with industrial action may also wish to consider taking measures against the organisers. This area of law is very complicated and employers would require expert advice on the facts of their case. We indicate the options available only very briefly.

Industrial Action and the Employment Relationship

Industrial action usually involves employees breaching their employment contracts. Banning voluntary duties, such as voluntary overtime, would not be a breach of contract. Going on strike, however, always is. This is so even when notice is given (unless it takes the form of collective resignation, which is highly unlikely). Striking is such a serious breach of contract that employers are entitled to dismiss strikers without notice. (See Chapter 19.) Other forms of industrial action, such as working to rule, banning compulsory overtime and blacking particular duties, are also breaches of contract. They involve breach of either express terms to perform specific tasks or the implied duty of co-operation. Whether or not employers can dismiss without notice depends on the seriousness of the breach. In practice, most employers do not want to dismiss in this situation; they want to secure a return to work. In this section, we look at other measures employers can take. We also look at the position of employees who are in fact dismissed in relation to unfair dismissal and redundancy.

Measures other than dismissal

One measure employers can take when faced with industrial action short of a strike is to send employees home without pay until they agree to work normally. They can also sue strikers and others taking industrial action in the civil courts for damages. The measure of damages will be the loss resulting from the breach of contract (see Chapter 16). In the case of production workers, this could be a substantial amount. For non-production workers, however, damages are limited to the cost of finding a replacement worker. In practice employers do not generally pursue this course.

Clearly sending workers home means that no work gets done at all. Can employers allow employees to continue working without performing all their duties and reduce their pay to compensate? This is a question to which the courts give different answers. On one view, the only remedy is to sue for damages. In two recent cases, however, the courts have allowed employers to deduct sums from wages provided that these amounts are not greater than the amounts employers could have claimed in damages. Under the Wages Act 1986, employers need not follow the notific-ation procedures if making deductions for this reason (see Chapter 18).

Industrial action and unfair dismissal

The Employment Protection (Consolidation) Act 1978 provides that in general the fairness of a dismissal cannot be examined where at the time of dismissal the employee was taking part in a strike or other industrial action, or the employer was conducting a lock-out. (A lock-out occurs when an employer refuses to allow employees to work because of a dispute.) This provision does not apply, however, where the employer discriminates between employees.

The industrial action need not involve a breach of contract for the general exclusion to apply. Industrial action is distinguished from refusals to work for other reasons, such as the desire to attend a football match, by its purpose. It is normally taken to put pressure on an employer to do something. Once employees have begun taking industrial action, they are assumed to continue doing so until they intimate otherwise. An employee who was on strike and then fell ill was still 'taking part' in the strike as he had not said anything to the contrary. Again, if employees refuse to cross a picket line without being physically stopped from doing so employers can assume they are taking part in the action. It may be different if they tell the employer they do not agree with the strike. It will clearly be different if they are absent for some other reason such as being on holiday.

If employers discriminate between employees taking industrial action, they lose their general protection. The dismissed employees can then claim unfair dismissal. Discrimination in this context may arise in one of two ways:

1 Where any other employee at the same establishment taking part in the action at the complainant's date of dismissal was not dismissed;
2 Where any other employee at the same establishment taking part in the action at the complainant's date of dismissal was offered re-engagement within three months of his or her dismissal and the complainant

was not. Re-engagement may be in the same job or a different 'reasonably suitable' one. Factors like status, skill and other benefits are relevant here. The job may be with the original employer or an associated employer.

In relation to a lock-out, employers lose their protection if they discriminate in these ways between employees whose terms of employment are likely to be automatically affected by the outcome of the dispute.

The fact that a tribunal is able to hear an unfair dismissal claim does not make the dismissal unfair; the normal principles then apply. It may be that an employee's misconduct during the dispute, such as damaging property, may justify dismissal.

Industrial action and redundancy payments

If employees receive notice of redundancy while they are on strike or taking any other industrial action which is a serious breach of contract, they are not entitled to redundancy payments. If they receive notice of redundancy and then go on strike, in general the right to a payment, or at least part of it, will still apply.

Strikes and continuity of employment

As Chapter 17 makes clear, weeks during which an employee is on strike or locked-out do not count for continuity purposes but continuity is still preserved.

Industrial Action and the Organisers

Employers faced with industrial action by their employees may have a remedy against the organisers. Industrial action nearly always involves the commission of a tort. The appropriate remedies, which must be sought in the ordinary civil courts, are injunctions and damages. An interlocutory injunction can be granted to halt a campaign pending a full trial.

Whether or not these remedies are available depends on whether the action is protected by the statutory 'immunities'. Industrial action is protected if it is taken 'in contemplation or furtherance of a trade dispute'. A 'trade dispute' is a dispute between workers and their own employer over one of a number of matters. These include terms and conditions of employment, the allocation of work, the engagement or dismissal of a worker, trade union membership or the lack of it, discipline, facilities for union officials, and negotiating machinery. In general, if action falls within this formula the employer has no remedy. Secondary industrial action, however, is not protected unless it satisifed stringent tests. Basically it must involve a first customer or first supplier of the employer in dispute. Immunity is also lost where action is 'official', that is, approved by a trade union, and no ballot has been held. A majority of those likely to participate in the action must have voted in favour of it.

Index

Peter F. Drucker
Management £3.95

Peter Drucker's aim in this major book is 'to prepare today's and tomorrow's managers for performance'. He presents his philosophy of management, refined as a craft with specific skills: decision making, communication, control and measurement, analysis – skills essential for effective and responsible management in the late twentieth century.

'Crisp, often arresting . . . A host of stories and case histories from Sears Roebuck, Marks and Spencer, IBM, Siemens, Mitsubishi and other modern giants lend colour and credibility to the points he makes'. ECONOMIST

The Practice of Management £3.95

'Peter Drucker has three outstanding gifts as a writer on business – acute perception, brilliant skill as a reporter and unlimited self-confidence . . . his penetrating accounts of the Ford Company . . . Sears Roebuck . . . IBM . . . are worth a library of formal business histories' NEW STATESMAN

'Those who now manage ought to read it: those who try to teach management ought to buy it' TIMES EDUCATIONAL SUPPLEMENT

William Kay
Tycoons £2.95

'I remember our bank sneering at Habitat when it started. They thought it was here today and gone tomorrow . . . . ' Sir Terence Conran

How do tycoons like Robert Maxwell and Sir Terence Conran make their fortunes? When did they decide to start out on their own? How did they begin? What attracted them to the competitive, exciting world of business. And what keeps them at it long after they've made more money than they could spend in several lifetimes? Do *you* have what it takes?

In this highly stimulating and above all instructive analysis of what makes top tycoons tick, William Kay, City Editor of *The Times*, charts the careers of thirteen of Britain's most successful entrepreneurs. In far greater depth than ever before, they explain to Kay how they got going, they reveal the secrets behind their continuing success, and they offer priceless advice to every aspiring tycoon who wants to take the plunge.

'In business, if you are persistent you normally arrive. It's the old tortoise and hare story. You don't have to be supergood . . . .' Noel Lister, MFI

David Ogilvy
Confessions of an Advertising Man £3.95

The Classic book on advertising

David Ogilvy is the doyen of advertising. The products he has advertised have been known to millions throughout the world since he started his agency in New York in 1949.

Confessions of an Advertising Man, first published in 1963, was a distillation of all the successful Ogilvy concepts, tactics and techniques – it rapidly became an international bestseller. Now, David Ogilvy has written an updating review of his industry to consolidate this revised edition of CONFESSIONS – published for the first time in Pan Books.

Confessions is the standard introductin to advertising, written in the bracingly robust style which has become the Ogilvy hallmark. It is the ideal 'how to' guide:

- How to acquire clients and keep them.
- How to be a good client.
- How to build strong campaigns.
- How to write potent copy.
- How to make television commercials.
- How to rise to the top of the tree.

Confessions is required reading for everyone in the advertising industry, from bottom to top.

Maurice Levi
Economics Deciphered £2.95

a survival guide for non-economists

Most people accept that economics is way beyond them; that discussion
of money supply, budget deficits, exchange rates, and inflation is solely
for the specialists. Here's a book for the general reader, offering in plain
English a clear appreciation of the principles and terminology of a subject
which affects every one of us. The lively question-and-answer format avoids
jargon and mathematics, explaining the key issues and offering an
understanding of the major ideas of leading economic thinkers such as Adam
Smith, Keynes, Galbraith and Friedman. Case examples illustrate the
importance and relevance of the discussion to everyday experience. An ideal
introduction.

Graham Mott
Accounting for Non-Accountants £3.95

A concise practical guide that provides salvation to non-accountant managers
baffled by the specialist terminology and complex figures of financial
statements and accounting practices. The logical coverage is backed up by
numerous examples and a detailed glossary of key words. *Accounting for
Non-Accountants* explains the major financial topics necessary for effective
business management.

Pan Management Guides

For executives who want to acquire
essential new management skills
to develop their careers

Pan Management Guides will give today's hard-pressed executives and
those who run their own businesses a more thorough grounding in
essential management skills, sufficient to enable them to run their
departments or businesses more effectively and successfully.

Pan Management Guides are written by authors who combine practical
international experience of their subject with deep background knowledge.
Each book in the series covers one crucial area of modern business so that
a complete library of vital information can be built.

Pan Management Guides are down-to-earth and uncluttered, designed to
enable you to quickly absorb only the facts that matter.

Books in the series:

Advertising and PR
Company Accounts
English in Business
Essential Law
Financial Management
Industrial Relations
Information Technology
Management Accounting
Management of Business
Marketing
Personnel Management
Production and Operations Management

All these books are available at your local bookshop or newsagent, or can be ordered direct from the publisher. Indicate the number of copies required and fill in the form below.

Send to: **CS Department, Pan Books Ltd., P.O. Box 40, Basingstoke, Hants.   RG21 2YT.**

or phone: 0256 469551 (Ansaphone), quoting title, author and Credit Card number.

Please enclose a remittance* to the value of the cover price plus: 60p for the first book plus 30p per copy for each additional book ordered to a maximum charge of £2.40 to cover postage and packing.

*Payment may be made in sterling by UK personal cheque, postal order, sterling draft or international money order, made payable to Pan Books Ltd.

Alternatively by Barclaycard/Access:

Card No.

Signature:

Applicable only in the UK and Republic of Ireland.

While every effort is made to keep prices low, it is sometimes necessary to increase prices at short notice. Pan Books reserve the right to show on covers and charge new retail prices which may differ from those advertised in the text or elsewhere.

NAME AND ADDRESS IN BLOCK LETTERS PLEASE:

....

Name————————————————————————

Address————————————————————————

————————————————————————————

————————————————————————————

————————————————————————————